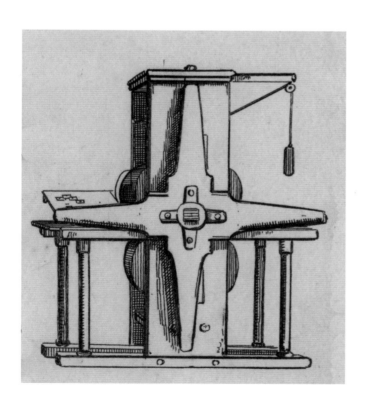

PRINTING THE TOY THEATRE

David Powell

J. R. Piggott, Horatio Blood

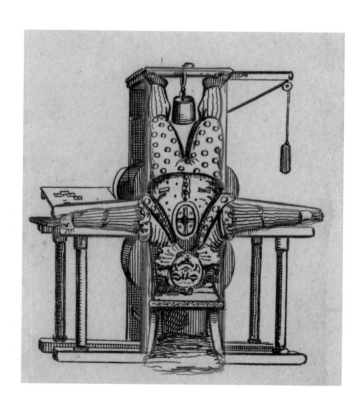

Pollock's Toy Museum Trust
2009

Published by Pollock's Toy Museum Trust,
in association with the exhibition
Printing the Toy Theatre at St Bride Library, London EC4
22 December 2006 to 4 January 2007

This publication has been generously supported by
The Marc Fitch Fund
The Barbara Whatmore Trust

© The authors
Designed by Julie Farquhar
Printed at Northend Press, Sheffield

ISBN 978-0-9564251-0-2

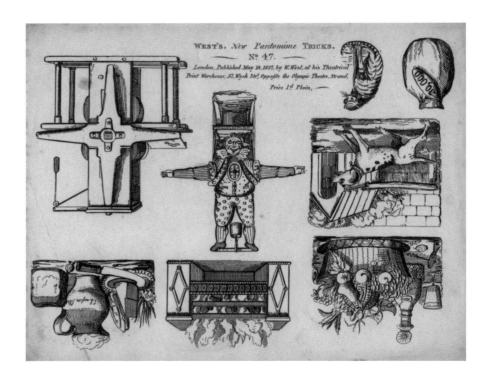

Half-title, title page and right: West's
Pantomime Tricks no. 47 (1827)
(David Robinson collection)

Copies available from the Trust at
99 Judd Street, London WC1H 9NE
www.pollocksmuseum.co.uk

INTRODUCTION

I don't know when my quest for copper plates (as used by the toy theatre publishers) began. I had realised that such things existed, ever since I read George Speaight's *Juvenile Drama*.[1] But it was many years before I set eyes on a plate, or held one in my hand, or acquired an instinctive feel for the size, shape and weight of the thing. My overmastering passion has always been for the printed sheets, for dating the undated among them, and for putting names (of artists and engravers) to those left unsigned. But on a visit to Pollock's in 1976 I met Roger Thompson, who was the first person there to take me seriously as a person or as an inquirer, and he showed me the copper and zinc plates, from which he was at that time doing some excellent printing. I started to wonder whether the differing material of the plates might be a clue that would help to sort engraver from engraver. This hunch was, as it turned out, completely misguided, but pondering on its possibilities kept up my interest for some years.

When I arrived in London in 1981, fresh from cataloguing the F. B. Brady Collection of theatricalia at Christ Church, Oxford, I was pounced on by Marguerite Fawdry, the presiding genius of Pollock's Toy Museum, who asked me to catalogue her own collection of prints. Although I made considerable progress with this, and made a start on the print collection of the museum also, the only work that I actually saw through to a finish was my catalogue of the archive of plates owned by Pollock's Toy Theatres Ltd.[2] I also managed to do a certain amount of printing, having been trained up to this by Debby Brown, Curator of the museum. In particular, I printed some copies of *Harlequin St George and the Dragon*, the last good set of which had been cut up to create the colour-printed version of that play. But at this point a mysterious illness struck, and all these things were abandoned. I particularly regret having stopped short of the point where I needed fresh printing materials, so that I never had to go to the suppliers in Bleeding Heart Yard and ask for "half a pound of heavy French". (Both Marguerite and Kenneth Fawdry were staunch supporters during my illness, he writing stiff letters to my doctor, who didn't seem to be doing much for me, and she presenting me with ancient packets of glucose, unearthed from the recesses of her kitchen cupboards.)

Although I tried to return to printing when I was well enough, I found I had lost the knack of it, and quickly gave up. For many years too I almost gave up my researches and writing, until at last my muse was reawakened by a commission from Barry Clarke, the *doyen* of Pollock's, to write Historical Notes for a series of facsimile reprints of toy theatre plays projected by him and underwritten by John Holt of Glasgow. Up to that time, Barry often used to lament his inability to inspire me to write. I hope that, half-a-dozen Notes and several catalogues later, he is more confident of his inspirational powers.

The work here presented is mainly based on my cataloguing of the Pollock archive (including the plates of Green, Redington and Park) more than twenty years ago. And I am most grateful for the opportunity of putting into print researches which I never thought anyone would be interested in. But when I was honoured by Laurie Webb with a commission to write *W. G. Webb and the Victorian Toy Theatre* for the Webb Festival of 2005, I was also entrusted with a draft of Laurie's own eagerly-awaited work on the Webb family, and with Geoffrey Judd's list of the Webb archive (including the plates of Webb, Skelt and Fairburn/Johnson, and more plates by Green). I have thus been able in what follows to present a less one-sided picture than I could otherwise have done, though, because the Webb archive (now held by the Cotsen Children's Library, Princeton University Library) is mostly unavailable for inspection, the level of detail on this side of things is still much thinner than I would wish to be the case. (But since I wrote these words, the situation has changed dramatically, and the staff of the library are now making the most determined efforts to prepare the archive for access.)

I should like to thank Alan Powers for having once again had a brilliant idea for an exhibition and seen it through to fulfilment. It would not have been possible without the enthusiastic partnership of the St Bride Library, especially Nigel Roche, Rob Banham and Catherine Dixon. Jan Piggott has been an enthusiastic and very patient colleague; and Horatio Blood, whom I involved in the proceedings at a very late stage, has supported my efforts and supplied my deficiencies with his customary energy and zeal, that is to say with far larger dollops of those qualities than I had any right to expect under the circumstances.

I should like to thank Peter Baldwin for submitting to my shameless raids on his unparalleled collection, David Robinson for giving unstinting access to so many of the plates without which the exhibition would be lacking its heart and soul, and the Executors of the late George Speaight, for giving us permission to borrow unique items from the Speaight collection. Among lenders of more specialised material, I should like to thank Hugo Brown, for giving ready consent to lend an important relic of his esteemed ancestor J. K. Green, and Kate Irvine, who with magical suddenness, and with cavalier in attendance, appeared bearing her dazzling gifts. And I should like to thank Barry Clarke, the most lavish of our lenders, for throwing himself into the preparations for the exhibition with a drive and enthusiasm surpassing even what we have come to expect of him.

Among institutions and their curators, I should like to thank Beverley Cook of the Museum of London for smoothing our path towards finding and borrowing plates and other items from the King Collection, and Cathy Haill of the Theatre Museum for presiding so helpfully and authoritatively over my day at Olympia, where I spent a most instructive time inspecting the museum's plates and blocks, including those of the Stone and Morice Collections.

This catalogue has been made possible by earlier donations from individuals to Pollock's Toy Museum Trust, and by a generous grant towards publication costs from the Marc Fitch Fund, with valuable support from Dr Brian Alderson and Professor Ian Christie.

D. L. P.

Abbreviations

In the plays,
    Plate 5 (of Characters): ch. 5
    Scene 2, No. 3: sc. 3
    Back of Scene 2, No. 4: sc. 4
    Plate 2 (of Tricks): tr. 2
    No. 17 (of Side Wings): wg 17

Among the portraits and miscellaneous sheets,
    No. 23 (in series): no. 23

Among the double plates (images side by side or head to head),
    Plate 1 + Plate 2 (of Characters): ch. 1/2
    Scene 2, No. 3 + Back of Scene 2, No. 4: sc. 3/4
    Plate 9 (of Characters) + Scene 6, No. 7: ch. 9/sc. 7
    No. 23 + No. 24 (in series): no. 23/24

With reference to collections,
    PB Peter Baldwin
    BC Barry Clarke
    KI Kate Irvine
    JP Jan Piggott
    PTMT Pollock's Toy Museum Trust
    DP David Powell
    AP Alan Powers
    DR David Robinson
    GS The late George Speaight, by permission of the Executors

Note on Paper Sizes

Although the first twenty years or so of the trade were more chaotic, from the 1830s to the 1930s the toy theatre publishers were remarkably consistent in the sizes of paper they used, these being only a fraction larger or smaller than the copper plates from which the sheets were printed. Thus, "halfpenny" publications were printed on paper about 8½ x 6½ inches, "penny" ones (when they were still offered) on paper about 9½ x 7½ inches, and large penny scenes (usually lithographic) on paper about 12½ x 10½ inches. Reprints of the halfpenny publications from the 1940s onward tended to be on slightly (but only slightly) larger sheets.

Standing apart from all this are twentieth-century impressions taken directly from the plates. These have traditionally been done on larger sheets of paper, to show off the plate mark. This is especially true of the prints made by Fores of Bond Street, which were done on hand-made paper of various, but usually extravagantly large, sizes. Maddeningly, some of the connoisseurs who purchased the Fores prints chose to cut them down to about a quarter of an inch wide of the plate mark. To say nothing of the vandalism involved, this sometimes makes the prints less easy to identify conclusively than would otherwise be the case.

PRINTING THE TOY THEATRE

David Powell

For half a century (1811–63, the lifetime of W. M. Thackeray) the toy theatre was one of the givens of English childhood. Sheets of hand-coloured characters and scenes were mounted on cardboard, and performances of all the latest plays and pantomimes were got up on miniature wooden stages in the Theatre Royal, Drawing Room. Until about 1832, the printed sheets were sold at the celebrated price of "a penny plain and twopence coloured", by West, Jameson, Hodgson, and any number of others. A new wave of publishers came along in the later 1820s, Dyer, Straker, Lloyd, and Park & Golding, who endeavoured to give better value for money by cramming more on to each sheet, and whose aesthetics palpably shifted towards those of popular art, as opposed to cheap high art. After that, the prices were halved, and though "a halfpenny plain and a penny coloured" has less of a ring to it, many times the number of sheets must have been sold at that price than at the more proverbial one. The publishers were now Park, Skelt, Green, Webb and Redington, but not many lesser names, for the business had become more cut-throat and monopolistic, requiring economies of scale before it even verged on the viable. By the early 1860s, the abolition of the remaining paper and advertisement taxes had enabled the proprietors of newspapers and magazines to deluge the public with cheap printed matter, and even halfpenny sheets now seemed expensive. Boys' magazines gave away characters and scenes free with each issue, and "penny packet" publishers, who also dealt in shadow figures and a whole range of cut-out paper toys, managed to put the gist of a whole play on to one large sheet of paper, sold for a single penny. By the 1880s, only two of the old guard

Detail of zinc plate from Green's *Blackbeard the Pirate* (1851), with Pollock's lithographic reprint, hand-coloured [1880s] (DR, AP)

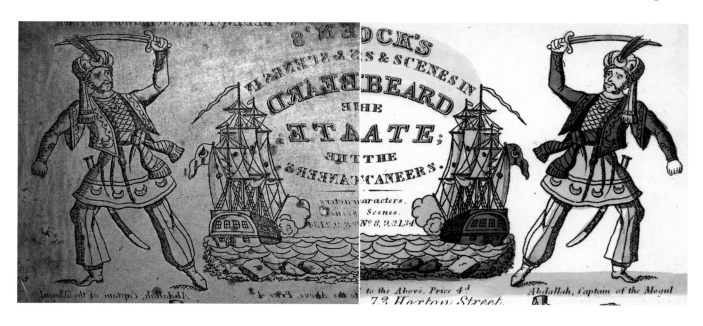

Here's thy Health in rosy Wine. | Command i'll fight to Please thee Still.
And here's a Cake I call divine. | For 'tis Twelfth Night or what you will.

Wrapper for sheet of Twelfth Night Characters, imprint cut off [1820s] (PB)

remained: Pollock in Hoxton, and Webb in Finsbury. The Webb business petered out in the 1930s, but in 1944 the Pollock one was translated to the West End, where it was run first by Alan Keen and then by Marguerite Fawdry.

Commercially, the toy theatre never stood quite on its own. Its immediate parent was the children's lottery print (sheets of little pictures with captions, to help in learning the alphabet), and these and other wares continued to be produced by the toy theatre publishers. Many types of print were produced in the same style of art, by the same artists, and in the same format, as the toy theatre sheets. Plates of soldiers and military bands were arranged just like the plates of characters, while cottage prints

Three figures from a sheet of Langley's Twelfth Night Characters, with Fairburn's imprint [c. 1837] (PB)

T TOTAL THOMAS

N

Why are Jews at a feast like a brewer in his brewery?

WINIFRED WIZARD

S

Read the following sentence

SERGEANT BUZ FUZ

P

Why are law officers like foot guards?

9

and designs for jig-saws closely resembled the sheets of scenery. "Scraps" combined features of both types, besides been often arranged like theatrical "fours" and "sixes". Some toy theatre publishers (such as Skelt) rarely strayed from their chosen territory, while others (such as Park or Fairburn) were tireless producers of valentines and Twelfth Night characters, dream books and songsters, children's chapbooks and little manuals of conjuring.

But the most significant sideline was the theatrical portrait, which developed rather slowly over the first decade of the toy theatre, before gathering steam during the 1820s and flourishing madly during the 30s, by which time the craze for "tinselling" the portraits had become very big business indeed. Although the toy theatre trade managed to recover from a very bad patch in the 1840s, the production of portraits never really took off again, except for a late flowering round about 1860, just before the entire trade collapsed for good. Nevertheless, where portraits were concerned, the 1830s peak had been unbelievably massive, with thousands of pounds of profit being ploughed back into the manufacture of dies and punches for tinsel-making. Nor was the full-size "single" portrait the only fish in the sea. In 1818 "combats" (the hero and villain of a play engaging in a sword-fight) suddenly came into popularity. Then in about 1830 "sixes" (six miniature portraits on a sheet) were strongly promoted by Park and Golding, with "fours" following close on their heels. Of other possible combinations, "pairs", "threes", "eights", "nines" and "tens" never caught on to the same extent, but "twelves" and "sixteens" were quite numerous during the last decade or so of the trade.

One of the most important characteristics of the English toy theatre, and the one that gives it its abiding historical importance, is the fact that its plays were all drawn from the contemporary London stage, of which they constitute a fifty-year record, unique in its breadth and depth of coverage. For the first few prints, the engravers relied on pre-existing illustrations, often of rather dubious relevance to their ostensible subject. But this phase passed away within months, and thereafter the toy theatre artists visited the theatre with notebook in hand, and worked up their sketches into finished designs when they got home. In the days of West and Hodgson, the artists frequently etched their own drawings on to copper plates.[3] This is reasonable enough, since etching is distinguished by being an artist's medium, not especially laborious, and requiring little specialised training. Etching your own work also means that you don't have to sit helpless while your efforts are spoiled by an incompetent or unsympathetic collaborator. The artist did not have to buy his own plates, as these were provided by the publisher,[4] who might then pay the artist £1 for his finished effort.[5] And West sometimes paid £1 10s. for work of

From top to bottom: labels for four packs of *Conversation Cards* [Green, *c.* 1845], printed by Edwin Smith (PTMT); cottage print issued by Green (1841), reversed from an earlier design by Park, printed by David Powell (DP); cover for a small children's book produced by Green [1850s], printed by Edwin Smith (PTMT); a sample of the endless variety of printed items produced by Redington [*c.* 1860] (PB)

unusual quality,[6] often raising the price of a plain sheet from 1*d.* to 1½*d.* in consequence. By the time of Orlando Hodgson (early 1830s), the artwork prepared for him by Robert Cruikshank seems more usually to have been handed over to other men for the etching, even though the artist was quite capable of doing this for himself. Thus, although his original drawings for both characters and scenes seem to be of a matching quality, when we come to the engraved versions, the characters have become animated almost to the point of lunacy, while the scenes are comparatively stiff and pedestrian. In the present state of research, it would be premature to generalise about the "halfpenny" period, but one's first impression is that the tendency towards division of labour (towards factory methods, if you like) almost certainly continued and increased. As to payment, though we have no direct information on the subject, comparison with other areas (such as playwriting) suggests that artists and engravers in this later period would have had to settle for much less than the £1 that West's proud young employees disdainfully accepted.

Lack of Records

When we wish to draw aside the veil that separates us from the men who drew, engraved, printed and published these things of so much beauty and fascination, and to glimpse something of their working lives, we are both rich and poor in our resources. Despite the survival of two large archives, the Pollock and the Webb, there is not a single account book, stock book, ledger, or anything of that kind to be found among them. (Until the Keen revival, that is, from which time onwards there is fairly copious material of this sort.) This is perhaps the more surprising on the Webb side of things, where even the pipes smoked by H. J. Webb have been dutifully preserved for posterity. As it is, when Henry Mayhew was shown West's ledgers in 1850, and reported a few details of their arrangement and contents, this would prove to be our first and last glimpse of such things.[7]

Preliminary Drawings

With regard to preliminary drawings, many more survive than was realised until recently, though as yet very little work has been done on them. Huge numbers of drawings survive in the Webb archive at Princeton, most of them apparently for projects that never came to fruition. Smaller numbers of drawings were bought from the Webbs in the 1930s by George Speaight and Gerald Morice,[8] and these seem more often to be for recognisable Webb or Skelt sheets. Some are rather lightly drawn (leaving quite

From top to bottom: original drawing, artist unknown, for a sheet of Horse Combats (PB); the finished sheet, as published by Hodgson and Co. (1823) (PB); rough sketches of theatrical subjects by Robert Cruikshank (signed for the benefit of a collector?) (PB); original drawing by Robert Cruikshank (unsigned) for a plate of characters in Orlando Hodgson's *Aladdin* (1832) (PB); Green's characters in *Aladdin* (1841), copied (but rearranged) from Orlando Hodgson (BC)

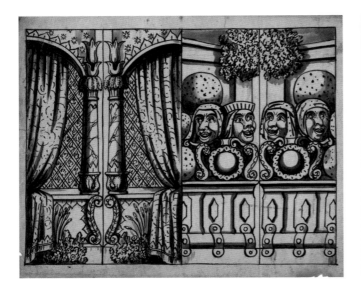

Original drawing for a plate of wings in Skelt's *Harlequin Cock a Doodle Doo* [*c.* 1837], with a hand-coloured copy of the finished print (PB)

a bit to the engraver's imagination), but many are so carefully worked out in pen and wash as to be almost a twin of the finished engraving. In the Webb archive many of the drawings show very early stages of the planning, with the sheets having no actual characters but only arrows showing which way the characters must face, and the names written underneath.[9] Marguerite Fawdry used to have in her collection the drawings for three plates of Green's *Wapping Old Stairs*, but hardly anything else from the Green-Redington-Pollock front has ever come to light.[10]

Many of the Skelt drawings are on paper whose verso is of a light reddish hue. When I first saw these, my immediate guess (which I find was also the suggestion of H. W. Whanslaw) was that the red backing was for some sort of carbon-paper effect, so that the engraver could trace through the design on to the wax-covered plate. But many of the drawings show no sign of having had this sort of pressure applied to them, and others only have it in a few places. So I now wonder whether the artist responsible for these drawings did not simply have a large supply of the sort of paper often used for endpapers in commercial bookbinding of the period. Both the pale red hue and the way that certain areas of the red have discoloured almost to black seem highly reminiscent of this sort of thing. On the other hand, the drawings appear to range from the beginning to the end of Skelt's creative period (1832–43), so the stock of paper must either have been very large or very frequently renewed from the same source.

Original drawing by Robert Cruikshank (signed) for one figure from a plate of fours (PB)

From the *incunabula* of the toy theatre, the Ralph Thomas Collection[11] has a fair number of West drawings, which tend to divide into drawings for published plays of his early years (often more exquisitely charming than the final engraved version) and drawings for unpublished later plays. The latter include William Heath's drawings for two plays by George Soane (*Mary the Maid of the Inn* and *The Falls of Clyde*) and for a rare excursion into playwriting by the villainous O. Smith (*Lolonois*). The transitional period is dominated by Robert Cruikshank, drawings by whom have appeared at auction over many decades with more frequency than one would have dared to predict. Although only some of Cruikshank's

drawings are for toy theatre plays (Orlando Hodgson), others are equally interesting in being for the non-theatrical work of publishers strongly associated with theatrical prints (Marks, Fairburn). We can thus see how the same style of drawing was applied to toy theatre prints, Twelfth Night characters, valentines, and the coloured frontispieces of fairy stories, dream books, and criminal biographies.

Original drawing and finished print of a plate of characters in Webb's *Harlequin Dame Crump* [1857/58?] (PB)

Printing Plates: Archives and Collections

When we come to the copper and other plates from which the toy theatre sheets were printed, we find that, although very few remain from the early heyday of the business, the survival of plates from the "halfpenny" period (early 1830s to early 1860s) is remarkable. To begin with the Pollock archive: John Redington's own plates mainly date from *c.* 1857–64. At the death of J. K. Green in 1860, Redington bought the bulk of the latter's stock of plates, which went back to 1832 (though not back to Green's Regency career), and the combined stock passed to Redington's son-in-law Benjamin Pollock in 1877. In 1880 Pollock acquired plates of *c.* 1835–42 from the Park family, who were going out of the toy theatre business. The entire Green-Redington-Park stock was bought from Pollock's daughters by Alan Keen in 1944, and became part of the stock of Benjamin Pollock Ltd (afterwards Pollock's Toy Theatres Ltd). It consisted of the plates for about 50 plays by Green (with a few portraits and miscellaneous items), 8 plays by Redington (with nearly all of his other publications), and 8 plays by Park (but nothing else out of the myriad sundries produced by that firm).

When, less than a decade later, Keen went bankrupt, his stock of plates and printed sheets was bought by Marguerite Fawdry. Unfortunately the collection of plates she bought was somewhat depleted, the absent plates being usually those of Green. In the 1940s the only plates reported missing had been some of those in *Richard the Third*.[12] But in the meantime a number of plates had been lent by Keen to Edwin Smith, who had not

Recto and verso of a sheet of drawings for one of Skelt's earliest plays, *The Charcoal Burner* [*c.* 1833] (PB)

From to to bottom: drawing for a scene in Skelt's *My Poll and my Partner Joe* [mid-1830s] (PB); West's *New . . . Borders and Ground Pieces* (1827), signed "TL" (Layton) (BC); portrait by J. L. Marks *The King's Champion giving the Challenge* [1820s?], signed "Marks fecit", printed direct from the plate (BC)

got round to returning them by the time of the bankruptcy, and died in 1971. These included almost complete sets of *The Wreck Ashore, Cinderella, Blackbeard the Pirate, Belphegor the Conjurer,* and *Whittington and his Cat,* as well as part of *The Sleeping Beauty,*[13] together with plates for valentines, conversation cards, jumping jacks and a view of the Crystal Palace. This group of material was put up for auction by Edwin Smith's widow Olive Cook in 1983, and was split up into three lots: copper plates, zinc plates, and miscellaneous zinc plates. Both lots of zinc plates were eventually acquired by David Robinson, and the single lot of copper plates by the Theatre Museum. Prints taken from many of the plates by Edwin Smith himself passed to the Trustees of Pollock's Toy Museum in 2002, by the bequest of Olive Cook.

But Keen also kept some of the plates as souvenirs, and offered others for sale. In 1949 those interested were invited to send for a list of plates available, though no list is known to survive, and there may not have been any takers. If any plates were dispersed in this way, very few have been recovered. Redington's plate of his own shop[14] was presented to Pollock's Toy Museum by H. C. Sage (the Hoxton postman)[15] *c.* 1958, and in 1984 Redington's three pantomime portraits[16] were bought by the museum from Keen's daughter. A Redington drop scene is in the Stone Collection at the Theatre Museum.[17] Among those plates which cannot currently be accounted for, the most puzzling involve three Green plays from which a "sample" of four plates seems to have been taken away at some point: in two cases (*The Miller and his Men* and *The Children in the Wood*) the "sample" is still missing;[18] in the other (*The Life of a Soldier*) the "sample" is present, but all the rest of the play, including the frontispiece, is missing.[19] (Was someone planning to do lithographic printing in the manner of Pollock, who used to transfer four small plates to one stone?) There are likewise missing a certain number of odd plates from various Green and Redington plays, especially frontispieces (including the famous engraved title page and frontispiece for *Jack Sheppard*). Anyone who can throw light on the whereabouts of any these plates would be performing a great service to toy theatre history.

The plates of W. G. Webb date from 1842–63, his lithographic stones from about 1860–90. When William West died in 1854, Webb managed to acquire the plate of one of his portraits, which he republished.[20] In 1860, on the death of J. K. Green, Webb, like Redington, bought some of his plates, though a much smaller quantity. In 1872, when E. Skelt finally gave up his attempt to revive the Skelt family business, Webb acquired many of their plates and original drawings, dating mainly from *c.* 1832–43. At a time more difficult to ascertain, Webb acquired from W. S. Johnson plates originally issued by Fairburn *c.* 1837–39 but mostly bearing the name of Johnson, who had re-published them *c.* 1860. The combined Webb–Green–Skelt–Fairburn stock passed to Webb's second wife Caroline in 1890, and a few years later to his son H. J. Webb. At the latter's death in 1933, the archive passed to his son "Young Harry", who in turn died in 1962. The collection, completely forgotten about, was given a home by H. J.'s granddaughter Vera Judd and her husband

Geoffrey, until it was auctioned at Sotheby's in 1994. The main bulk (including all the Webb and Skelt plates, with some by Green) was bought by Justin Schiller, the well-known children's book dealer, for acquisition by the Cotsen Children's Library.[21] Small parts passed into private hands, including the Johnson plates, the bulk of Webb's Green plates, some plates of sixes by Bishop, and two portrait plates assumed to be anonymous but actually by Skelt. All these plates were bought by David Robinson, who thus comes to possess the third most important archive of toy theatre plates in the world. Mr Robinson also possesses further plates by Bishop and a plate by West's hated rival, Creed. Because the plates were divided up rather mechanically, Green plates altered by Webb to his own name and imprint were kept as part of the main (Princeton) archive, while unaltered plates were not; and obvious Skelt plates were kept, while ones from which the imprint had been removed were allowed to leave. But the whereabouts of all of them are known, and that is the main thing.

The Webb archive (Princeton branch and Robinson branch reckoned together) contains the plates for 19 original plays by Webb (and for as many as 7 unpublished plays[22]), one play partly adapted from Green[23] (plates unaltered), two plays adapted from Skelt[24] and one intended to be adapted[25] (plates unaltered), one play in process of being adapted from Skelt[26] (with, in this case only, the plates altered), and 15 other plays by Skelt (14 halfpenny[27] and one penny, ex Lloyd[28]), also assorted scenes and wings from other plays by Skelt. The archive further contains the plates for Webb's various stage fronts, orchestras, drop scenes, top drops and foot pieces, pantomime characters and tricks, portraits, fours, sixes, combats, scraps, soldiers, and comicalities, for a similar range of Skelt items (plates unaltered, with very rare exceptions[29]), and for a smaller number by Green (some plates altered, other not), Fairburn/Johnson (unaltered by Webb) and Bishop (unaltered). For Webb's own plates, the sequences are not always complete, though those plates that are missing have been missing for a very long time, with prints from them being now rare or even non-existent. The most annoying gaps are in the sequence of portraits, since surviving plates might have helped to solve certain problems to do with withdrawal, substitution and re-numbering that bedevil the main series of halfpenny portraits published from Cloth Fair in 1843–44. As it is, in seeking solutions to the puzzles they present, we are thrown back on our own powers of deduction and imagination. For the Skelt plates, the sequences are substantial, but never anything like complete. What we have here is a magnificent ruin, a broken but imposing fragment of the mighty Skelt archive that must have existed up to about 1862, before being dispersed, never to be reassembled.

Another long-standing archive is that of Jonathan King, presented to the Museum of London in 1912. King was a major producer of valentines and Christmas cards, and the son of one of Green's agents. His copper plates include two of the missing plates from Green's *Richard the Third*,[30] a portrait plate by W. Smith, and a number of portrait plates by J. L. Marks, together with some scene plates by Hodgson and Co., which came to King via Marks. King did a fair bit of printing from his Marks plates,

Above: three scenes from Lloyd's *The Pilot* [*c.* 1829, reprinted by Skelt *c.* 1834], signed "E Blake sc" (BC); and detail of Blake's signature from a scene in *The Dumb Savoyard and his Monkey*, originally published by Straker 1828, then Lloyd [*c.* 1830], then Skelt [*c.* 1834] (BC)

Top left: detail of zinc plate of tricks in Green's *Whittington and his Cat* (1853) (DR); *top right*: zinc plate of characters in the same pantomime, showing information removed from Pollock's lithographic reprint (DR); *middle*: Green portrait *Mr E. F. Saville as Jack Sheppard* (1839) (BC); *bottom*: Green's *Combat in Jack Sheppard* (1849), impression taken from the plate by H. J. Webb [1920s?] (BC)

though he seems not to have printed directly from them (perhaps this was too passé by the time he acquired them). Instead he used lithographic transfer to make his prints, multiple copies of which (both plain and coloured) survive in his collection. And indeed similar multiple copies of other prints suggest that King may once have possessed a much larger selection of plates than now remain in the collection that bears his name.

The Theatre Museum possesses three groups of plates: those that came with the M. W. Stone Collection (presented 1955), those that came with the Gerald Morice Collection (acquired after his death), and those that were bought by the Museum from Phillips in 1983. Stone Collection Box 30 contains a number of Skelt penny and halfpenny plates[31] and Skelt (ex Lloyd?) penny plates[32]. It also contains three Green plates[33] and a Redington drop scene[34]. Some of the Skelt plates may have come to Stone from the Webb family archive; the Redington plate was perhaps bought from Alan Keen; the Green items could have come from either source. The F. B. Brady Collection, Christ Church, Oxford, includes one copper plate, given to Mr Brady by Mr Stone. It is a plate of Skelt's penny sixes (ex Lloyd?).[35] The Brady Collection also has impressions of this and most of the other Stone plates, printed on large sheets of good-quality paper, so it seems likely that Stone commissioned these pulls and circulated them among his friends. Indeed, one example belonging to a well-known London collector has a contemporary pencil endorsement to the effect that it was printed in 1951, with six impressions only being taken, and two each given to Desmond Seaton-Reid, Brady, and Stone himself.

Morice Collection Box 139 and Box 154 contain the complete set of plates for Skelt's *The Floating Beacon*, all done on the back of old caricatures. There are also plates by Bishop, many altered from Carr, and many of the single ones showing signs of being cut up from double ones: 10 por-

traits, one pair, one plate of sixteens, and two plates of miniature soldiers. In addition, there are Green's halfpenny equestrian portrait no. 9, a large portrait by Morrish, and a plate purporting to be Dyer's portrait of Kean as Hamlet. This last is probably a forgery, and is suspicious on three grounds: it is zinc, its lettering is not the work of a professional calligrapher, and its imprint seems to have been copied from another plate by Dyer[36], but with the original date 1826 (the earliest year that Dyer is known to have been in business) misread as 1820. There are also two plates with no obvious toy theatre connections: a satire on Kean's affair with Mrs Cox, signed by Fores, and a penny-sized plate, with six little oriental scenes. According to Morice himself,[37] his plates (including those for *The Floating Beacon*) were found, during the summer of 1936, "in the basement of a well-known bookshop in the Charing Cross Road". He also possessed woodblocks for shadow figures, found on a stall in the Farringdon Road about 1938, but these (apart from one block of characters in *Cinderella*) do not seem to be preserved in the collection.[38]

A considerable number of Skelt plates were offered for sale during the 1980s and 90s, though their provenance was never very clear. Many, bought in 1996 at a Phillips sale in Oxford,[39] are now in the possession of Peter Baldwin, though he has sold others to fellow-collectors.

George Speaight had one copper plate (now in the Robinson collection), for a sheet of Skelt (late Lloyd?) penny sixes[40], re-using part of the verso of a threepenny plate by Hodgson[41], cut down to the size needed. But the older image seems to have been squashed flat in the process of preparing the new surface, and does not look as if it could now be printed

Two portraits originally produced by Fairburn (1837–38), altered for reissue by Johnson [*c.* 1860], and here reprinted direct from the plates, and coloured, by H. J. Webb [1920s?]

Two penny portraits by Green [*c.* 1835], afterwards converted to halfpenny ones (1849), impressions taken from the plates and coloured by H. J. Webb [1920s?] (BC)

from. The Barry Clarke collection also has one copper plate, Skelt late Lloyd's portrait no. 18, *Miss Paton as Rebecca in the Maid of Judah.* (For more details, see page 17 with note 54.) The present author's collection has, apart from five double plates by Skelt, the zinc plate for an equestrian portrait by Green,[42] forming a pair to one previously part of the Webb archive and now in the Robinson collection.[43] My zinc plate cannot definitely be traced to the Webbs, but has certainly belonged to someone able to do lithographic transfers and willing to distribute them, since one lithographic print (with much of the lettering removed, but restored in pencil) accompanies the plate, and a print of identical description, formerly owned by George Speaight, is in the Robinson collection.

Printing Plates: Publishers and Periods

It thus comes about that substantial quantities of the plates of all five major publishers of the "halfpenny" period survive into the twenty-first century, in two main archives: the Green, Redington, and Park plates in the Pollock archive (intact until the 1940s, but then partially dispersed); and the Webb, Skelt and Green plates in the Webb archive (intact until 1994, and then partially dispersed). When the Robinson collection is taken into account, there is very little that cannot be accounted for on the Webb side of things; on the Pollock side, there are still a number of plates that need to be located, though even these are not as numerous as once seemed to be the case.

Other survivals from this later period include plates for the portraits of

Fairburn 1837–39, mostly altered to Johnson *c.* 1860, and important because of their frequent use as vehicles for tinselling (Robinson collection ex Webb). There are also about 20 portrait plates of Bishop 1850s?, many taken over from R. Carr 1840s?? (Robinson collection ex Webb and elsewhere; Morice Collection), a few of Marks 1830s (King Collection), and one of W. Smith 1835 (ditto). For Lazarus *c.* 1835 there is one combat surviving intact[44], and various other plates, including one portrait[45], one whole play[46], and a number of scenes[47], altered by Green to his own use (Pollock archive).

If it were not for the chance survival of the one copper plate still bearing his name, E. Lazarus would not be so much an obscure figure (which he still is), but almost an unknown one. As a toy theatre publisher he only flourished (if that is the word) from about 1834, when he registered a press, to 1836, when he must have sold his little stock of copper plates to Green, though he was still practising as a wood engraver at the end of the decade. As it is, he is interesting for being an "Ornament Maker" at least as early as James Webb, and for being perhaps the supreme representative of that Jewish involvement with the toy theatre which has remained either unnoticed or else noticed in the wrong places. (The Skelts have repeatedly been claimed as Jewish, though they were actually Huguenots; and the same has also been assumed, less often but equally wrongly, of the Pollocks.) But there is a fascinating procession of Jewish publishers, none of the first importance but including a number of significant figures. Here is the amiable rogue John Lewis Marks, his wife Sarah and their sons, a family enterprise which began in the era of West and ended in that of the penny packets; Suzman, the artist who was once a partner of Bailey and who afterwards worked for Webb, and left cheeky notes on his drawings for portraits ("We must give them something for their money, don't yer know!"[48]); Moss Hyams, Green's agent in Mint Street, Borough, in the early 1850s; and highly respectable Myers and Co., with their premises in Leadenhall Street and Berners Street, and their commercial links with Vienna and Berlin. But with Lazarus we seem to hit an early peak of this sort of thing. His very name, Eleazar Lazarus, the same appellation in Hebrew and Greek, seems to assert pride of race. And among the plates he has left behind is one for *Mr. Palmer as King Ahasuerus in the Triumph of the Jewish Queen.* This play was written by Elizabeth Polack, a member of a literary Jewish family which had befriended the singer Braham in his impoverished early days; it was written for performance at the Pavilion Theatre, Whitechapel, of all London theatres the one with the largest Jewish clientele; and it was not merely a play with a Jewish subject, but practically a Purimspiel, being given its first performance at Purim 1835, with illuminated wishes for a happy Purim burning bright as the curtain fell.

Bishop, like Lazarus, is not a publisher to whom one would have given much thought, were it not for the survival of a score or so of his plates. He is very difficult to date. Speaight lists him as a penny packet publisher of *c.* 1870, eventually taken over by Sarah Marks. But there are lithographic portraits from the late 1850s and ordinary ones from the late

Top: portrait by J. L. Marks [1830s?], in a lithographic printing by Jonathan King, hand-coloured [*c.* 1900?] (GS); *bottom*: portrait by J. L. Marks (1839), in a lithographic printing by Jonathan King [*c.* 1900?] (BC)

1820s (these could be taken over from someone else, but would have been rather old-fashioned by thirty years or so later). His surviving plates (as G. Bishop and Co., Houndsditch) contain some images which cannot predate the 1850s, but others are more suggestive of the 1830s. Many of the plates seem to be taken over from R. Carr (same address), but these too seem to extend from the mid-30s to the early 50s, so that it is difficult to suggest any plausible date for a changeover. Some of the designs are evident copies of portraits by Webb, sixes by Park, and sixteens by Green. Most of the plates are double ones sliced up rather badly to create single ones, and some are very lightweight and flimsy. What does all this mean? More research is needed here.

From the first twenty years of the trade very few plates survive. I have elsewhere conjectured that the plate of "the first cheap theatrical print", as invented and engraved by Green and published by West in 1811, does survive somewhere.[49] One plate by West certainly survives (Webb Archive), as well as one by his annoying neighbour Creed (Robinson collection, history unknown). A particularly surprising survival is plate 1 of the procession in *The Tiger Horde*, as published 8 Sep 1814 by Green & Slee, a plate whose verso was used by Lloyd 1829 for *Black Eyed Susan* sc. 1. Lloyd's plate was re-published by Skelt and then passed to Webb. Its journey so far has taken in Bishopsgate, Lambeth, Stepney, Finsbury, Salisbury, Poole, and New Jersey.

Two plates by Hodgson and Co. *c.* 1822 survive (King Collection), one cannibalised by Marks and one still intact. The plates of Hodgson and Co., after being taken over by Cole and then Maunder, seem to have been widely distributed, Fairburn acquiring some of the better portraits, while some of the other material passed through Dyer and perhaps thence to Skelt. (But the Skelt large scenes in *The Mountaineers*, commonly stated to be ex Dyer ex Hodgson, seem only to be ex Dyer.) Some of Hodgson's non-theatrical plates even turn up in books issued many years later by provincial presses. J. L. Marks may well have had many Hodgson plates, though he presumably didn't think them worth re-issuing. What came to King was a rather forlorn little penny scene in *Life in Paris*, together with one of Hodgson's justly-famed "large threepenny" scenes (in *Edward the Black Prince*), which, however, Marks had chopped up to make two double plates, using the blank sides for his (admittedly magnificent) set of four pantomime portraits.

Two plates by F. Edwards (1825–26) survive in the Webb archive, W. G. Webb having engraved scenes 7/8 and 9/10 of his *Miller in his Men* on their versos. The Webbs seems to have possessed one or more plates of characters from Edwards's version of the play (H. J. Webb printed them for collectors), so probably these were what he re-used; but the character plates might also have been on the back of Skelt plates in the Webb collection. Two Edwards designs (first and last scenes in *The Innkeeper's Daughter*, 1825) definitely survive on the back of Skelt plates in other collections.[50]

So much for the early period. As in other respects, the transitional publishers (Dyer, Straker, Lloyd, Park & Golding) fare surprisingly badly. Of the hundreds of "Skelt late Lloyd" plates that must once have existed

(many of them being indeed Skelt late Lloyd late Straker), very few seem to survive, and the selection that does remain seems very odd and accidental. In the Webb collection one complete play survives, the Skelt late Lloyd *Mazeppa*, together with the Lloyd scene in *Black Eyed Susan* mentioned above, two scenes from the Skelt late Lloyd *Mary the Maid of the Inn* (sc. 9, 11), two Sky Scenes (one in *The Miller and his Men*), and two plates of Wings (nos 14 and 15, Curtain and Gothic). The plate of Skelt [late Park & Co.] wings in *The Children in the Wood* no. 1 may well be the only surviving plate by Park & Golding. One portrait plate originally published by Straker survives: *Miss Hargrave as Amy Canzonette in Antoine the Savage.*[51] Some plates of pantomime characters are Skelt ex Dyer, as is a complete set of large scenes in *The Silver Palace*. In the Baldwin collection there are a plate of set pieces from Skelt's late Lloyd's *One O'Clock* (sc.10), the banquet scene from Skelt's penny *Wood Daemon*, and various other Skelt penny plates.[52] In the Stone Collection are various things already enumerated.[53] And in the Barry Clarke collection there is another Skelt late Lloyd portrait plate, which also seems likely to go back to Straker: *Miss Paton as Rebecca in the Maid of Judah.*[54] But this is a very thin haul, considering the importance of what it represents. One would have at least expected a complete set of plates for the Skelt late Lloyd *Mary, the Maid of the Inn* to have survived, not just a few odd ones, since this play is often found with the imprint of E. Skelt, and ought to have passed to Webb. Were these the things that W. G. Webb threw away against the wishes of his son H. J. Webb?[55]

The disappearance of penny plates contemporary with (or only a little older than) so many surviving halfpenny plates is certainly unfortunate. But the economics of the 1850s and 1860s, which made even halfpenny sheets seem rather expensive, meant that the old penny plates (which Park and Skelt held in large numbers, and Green and Webb to a smaller extent) had to pass through a period when the sheets printed from them seemed ever less saleable. Green, for example, gradually withdrew his penny plays, portraits and other sheets from sale, and he probably discarded most of the plates. Of his penny portraits, two were cut down and re-issued as halfpenny ones[56]. Of those penny plates still surviving at Green's death, some were cut down by Redington with a view to using their versos[57], and only a handful now survive in their pristine form[58], perhaps more by accident than design. Nor did the penny stock of other publishers escape the same treatment. Skelt cut down penny portraits to make halfpenny ones, sometimes altering the actor's name to someone more up-to-date in the process.[59]

Nevertheless, when we compare the disappearance rate of plates for other types of work with that of plates for the toy theatre, the fact that so much survives in so few archives seems almost miraculous. Dangers have always threatened on every side, as the melting down of the royal Hogarth plates during the Great War, the distribution of the last surviving set of Dickens plates and blocks to subscribers of the Nonesuch Dickens in 1937, and the blitzing of the plates for Harrison Ainsworth's novels during the Second World War, remind us. And we realise what a lot we owe to two stubborn old men in the early twentieth century and to their plucky descendants in the 1940s.

Copper and Zinc Plates

Of the plates that survive, copper is certainly the "typical" material, but zinc is more often used than Speaight allowed, and steel, so far from being not used at all (as he thought) turns out to be a favourite with some publishers also.[60] All the surviving plates by Park and Marks are copper, as are the few that survive from publishers pre-1830. The comparatively few plates by the Skelts that I have examined personally have been copper, and there is no positive evidence that they ever used anything else. For although there exists a much larger number of Skelt plates (*viz*, in the Webb Archive) that might conceivably turn out to be steel or zinc, the silence of the Judd lists is probably to be taken as indicating copper.[61] Green used copper plates throughout the 1830s, but in December 1839 he made a fatal change. Moralists always warned that the glamour surrounding *Jack Sheppard* would lead young men astray, and Green (though about to hit fifty) was no exception. The play was running at half the theatres of London, and a toy theatre version seemed essential. But the thing was an epic, requiring 64 sheets of characters and scenes (the largest quantity ever found in a juvenile drama), while its lengthy script cried out for the dignity of an engraved title page as well as the usual frontispiece. The capital outlay was more than Green had ever been faced with before, and he solved this problem by changing to the cheaper material of zinc. This proved so satisfactory (in his own eyes) that he continued to use zinc until his death in 1860. Not everyone would have agreed. When Redington became Green's agent in the early 1850s, he got Green to design and print a number of stage fronts, act drops and orchestras under Redington's name and imprint. At first the plates for these were of zinc, but later change to copper. (Admittedly one of these later ones was the "large Redington" stage front, which may have been too large for zinc to be practicable.) In 1857/58 Green and Redington quarrelled, and Redington started to produce plays on his own. He always used copper, and when he bought up Green's stock of plates in 1860, he referred to them in advertisements as "copper-plates", ignoring the fact that two-thirds of them were zinc. By the 1940s some of the zinc plates were showing signs of deterioration, as prints made by Edwin Smith reveal, and when the Pollock plates were put into storage during the early 1950s (allegedly coated with Vaseline and wrapped in corrugated cardboard) the zinc ones reacted badly with their damp environment while the copper ones came through unscathed. Nearly all the zinc plates are now damaged: some of them very lightly but others much more severely.

Steel Plates

It used to be thought that steel plates were not used in the toy theatre. Certainly there are none in the Pollock archive. But the Webb collection throws a different light on the matter, since it suggests that by the later 1830s the firm of Fairburn were using single steel plates to the exclusion of any other type. Moreover, W. G. Webb himself, whose plates mainly date from the period 1842–63, made intermittent use of steel, taking his cue as much from Fairburn (whose establishment he doubtless knew his way around) as from Park, to whom he had been apprenticed, and who invariably used copper.[62] The first two penny portraits issued by Webb from Cloth Fair (1843) were done on single steel plates,[63] but the sixth and last of the series was done on a copper one.[64] The frontispieces for his first two playbooks (1847–48)[65] were done on a steel plate, as was that for *The Battle of Alma* (1855?). His six Crimean War portraits were done on double steel plates,[66] and so were his four plates of sixteens (difficult to date).[67] The plates for *The Miller and his Men* (1862?) present a bewildering mixture of steel, copper and re-used copper.[68]

At least one publisher used the process of *engraving* on steel, and made a point of advertising the fact. Thus we get "Marks's New Series Engraved on Steel", from which prints of no. 7 *Mr. C. Kemble as Edgar in King Lear* can be found in more than one collection, but how much further the series got, or what date is to be put on it, is not clear. (Charles Kemble gave his "farewell" performances in 1836.)

Size of Plates

Between "penny" and "halfpenny" sheets there is one important difference. The "penny" ones are on full-sized quarto plates (10 by 8 inches) and the "halfpenny" ones on a reduced version of the same thing (9 by 7 inches). These sizes are adhered to fairly precisely by Green and Redington, and as a rule their plates vary from these proportions by no more than one-eighth of an inch. (It is important not to reduce the measure-

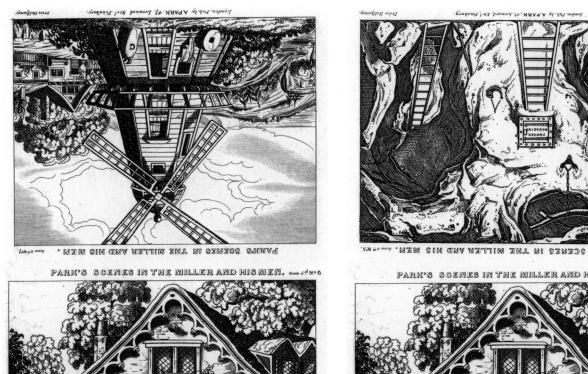

Two double plates from Park's *The Miller and his Men* [mid-1830s], showing accidental repeat of the "Flask" scene: modern printing from the plates by Fores of Bond Street (BC)

ments to a decimal equivalent, as this turns something meaningful into something arbitrary.) The plates of Skelt and Webb are consistently smaller than those of Green and Redington by about a quarter of an inch all round, say 8½ by 6½ inches. In practice two "plates" were frequently engraved on one double-sized (or folio) piece of copper (10 by 16 inches for two penny sheets and 9 by 14 or 8½ by 13½ for two halfpenny ones). I shall call these plates *double plates*, referring to surface area, rather than the double-sided use of both recto and verso, a subject to which we will come in due course. Although the only surviving West plate is single, double plates were very frequently used by him, as is shown by surviving prints (notably in the Thomas Collection, British Museum), where the two halves are still joined, with an engraved line between them for cutting along. With the publishers whose plates survive in large numbers, Park consistently uses double plates, while Green and Redington consistently use single ones. Skelt uses both, with perhaps a shift from double to single in mid-career and then back to double. For Webb, double plates were once again the norm. But this analysis mainly refers to the "halfpenny" work of the big five. When producing penny work, even those who otherwise favoured double plates seem to have preferred single ones. In this they differed from at least some of the older publishers.

Among the surviving prints of West (especially in the Thomas Collection), many conjoined pairs can still be found. These might be from his unsold stock, but equally he may sometimes have sold his prints uncut, since the sheets are engraved side by side and look very impressive. Conjoined pairs of Park, Skelt or Webb are not so common, but cut sheets often have above the title a line for cutting along (which has been ignored, and the sheet sliced centrally). The Skelt lines are particularly thick and conspicuous. Presumably the prints of this period were not sold uncut, as their orientation had now changed, so that the images were no longer engraved side by side, but head to head. This was for the convenience of the engraver, who never had to reach over more than half the length of his plate at a time, but the resulting print was not really aesthetically satisfying until cut into two.

Double plates have a number of implications for the contents of the artwork as well as for its technique. With portraits, they reinforce the tendency for prints to be produced in pairs or even sets of four. (Commercial greed and a feeling for symmetry obviously play their part in this, as well.) Thus a popular actor will be represented in two contrasting parts, or two thematically-connected parts, or in the same part "first and second dress". A classical play will be represented by two popular actors or actresses in the same role. A successful new play will be represented by hero and heroine, hero and friend, hero and villain, or villain and henchman. An unusually popular play will be represented by hero, heroine, villain and henchman, or some such combination. Even prints of a more self-contained type, such as combats, fours or sixes, tend to come in evenly-numbered series.

But there was a down-side to double plates. The toy theatre, like the real one, made regular use of stock scenes (such as forests, cottages, palaces, and so on), which could be used in play after play. Even more so with the sheets of wings. But if one scene of a pair joined head to head turned out to be widely useful, and the other was only suitable for the play from which it originally came, what was to be done? This must have been a problem for Park, who in his "halfpenny" work was the most determined user of double plates. With his scenes, he simply used no stock scenes at all (though he had used them remorselessly in his "penny" plays published with Golding). With his wings, either he must have been left with piles of unsaleable half-sheets (but I cannot think this would have been tolerated) or else he must have found a way of printing half a plate at a time. In the case of his first two plates of wings (1 and 2, and 3 and 4), where there was much less call for nos 2 and 4, he had a new version of 1 and 3 engraved in what the manufacturers of gramophone records used to call an "alternative coupling". One unexpected hazard of double plates appears in the scenes of Park's *Miller and his Men*, where sc. 6 (the "Flask" inn) has accidentally been engraved twice, once paired with sc. 5 and once with sc. 7. How could an engraver make such a glaring error, involving himself in fruitless effort and risking the wrath of his employer?

Characters from Park's *Der Freischutz* [early 1840s], showing long necks and no necks (DP)

My own explanation is that the work must have been put aside for a time, and that, when it was resumed, a scribbled note to the effect that the engraving had got as far as sc. 6 was misinterpreted. On the other hand, Barry Clarke once asked Marguerite Fawdry why the engraver should have acted as he did, and she gaily replied, "Drunk, darling!", a theory which some of my coarser readers may even prefer.

Techniques of Engravings

Sometimes the etched plate might have bits of pure engraving added for more delicate effects. In particular, we know this to be the case with Park, to whom W. G. Webb was apprenticed 1835–42 (almost exactly the period when Park was producing his halfpenny plays). Park was evidently rather vain of his own engraving skills, and, according to Webb, "always insisted on drawing the faces of the characters himself in drypoint" to the figures etched by his employees.[69] Although his heads are well drawn, they are often added in slightly the wrong place, so that the characters end up with necks elongated or non-existent. To have a master who marred your work under pretence of mending it must have been infuriating.

The use of stipple to give tones to the flesh is one of the distinguishing features of the character sheets, and was used by nearly all the publishers from West to Redington. But Green, ever the innovator, gave up the use of stipple in the early 1850s, and substituted cross-hatching, so that all of his plays from *Harlequin Oliver Cromwell* to *Goody Goose* (only excepting *The Daughter of the Regiment*, where the smallness of the characters necessitates a return to stipple) achieve the highly-stylised look associated with his later publications: cross-hatched faces, eyes drawn in too much detail, and rather sprawling bodies. It doesn't sound promising, but the results, as we all know, are glorious.

Another refinement was known as "stopping out". The plate was etched for a portion of the time deemed necessary, then part of the design (the more distant area of a landscape, for instance) was covered over, and etching was recommenced until the full time was completed. The stopped-out part of the scene would appear faint, thus adding to the effect of perspective. Many Skelt plates make good use of this process.

A technique rare on toy theatre sheets (but not so rare as used to be thought) is aquatint. In the outside world it was often entrusted to a specialist (other than the etcher of the overall design). Thus, in his work for the military publisher Jenkins, William Heath always claims credit for the etching, but says that the aquatinting is by Mr Stadler (or whoever it might be). In his theatrical work for West, there is never any aquatinting, and West would probably have thought it an expensive luxury. But from about 1820 aquatinting was sometimes used by other toy theatre artists and publishers for sky scenes, or even for the little bit of sky that can be seen through a door or window. This was perhaps done in order to make the scene (or part of a scene) work as a transparency, the effect being copied from the "protean" views published by Spooner and others. The technique makes its way into portraits, too, perhaps merely to increase their impressiveness. Thus in Park's two portraits of Master Owen as Young Norval[70], the penny one has aquatinting, though the halfpenny one is a simple etching.[71]

Lettering

The engraved (not etched) lettering of toy theatre plates was nearly always added to the finished art-work by a specialist calligrapher, using ruled lines, which if drawn too deeply would sometimes show up on the finished print. We may contrast this with the methods of caricature, where the etcher usually did his own lettering, in a freehand (and often

Below left: plate of characters in Green's *Douglas* (1834), showing delicate use of stipple (BC). *Below right*: plate of characters in Green's *Whittington and his Cat* (1853), showing the replacement of stipple by cross-hatching (PTMT). *Above*: details from the two plates

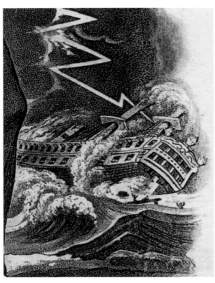

Mr Braham as Tom Tug Singing the Bay of Biscay, portrait (with much aquatinting) originally published by Fairburn [1836] and altered for re-issue by Johnson [*c.* 1860], impression taken from the final state of the plate, probably by H. J. Webb [1920s?], with his colouring; and detail from a similar impression, plain (BC)

wobbly) imitation of the calligrapher's art. This arrangement made twofold sense: since the content of a caricature was frequently ultra-topical, time could usefully be saved by cutting one stage out of the production process, while the informality of the lettering helped to give the prints the unbuttoned look which was part of their appeal. Though the toy theatre prints, with their connection to the contemporary stage, were semi-topical, time was obviously not thought to be the deciding factor, and the great majority have been elegantly lettered by calligraphers. The most notable exceptions are the "large threepenny" scenes drawn by George Childs for Hodgson & Co., which are lettered in the artist's own wayward hand. Since none of Hodgson's other work is lettered in this way, this must have been the artist's personal whim, tolerated in one whose work was so much above the common order. And some of Marks's portraits are lettered by the etcher-publisher himself. (But Marks was also a caricaturist.) Conversely, in the caricature world, the scurrilous publications of Fairburn are frequently graced by formal lettering. (But Fairburn was a publisher with many strings to his bow, including theatrical portraiture.)

The choice of calligraphic style is an important element in the overall house style of each publisher. Some publishers, such as Green, chose their style from the very beginning and stuck to it. Others, such as Park and Skelt, took a little time to settle down, initially plumping for the style later associated with the other house, but after a short time swapping horses in mid-gallop. (My metaphor is drawn from some Astley's Amphitheatre of the mind, rather than any more mundane species of equitation.) Redington was the most changeable, being determined to be fashionable, and inflicting on his reprints of Green's sheets a quintessentially mid-Victorian species of "artistic" lettering, ill-suited to their late-late-Regency aesthetic. But Pollock, as we shall see, had ideas of his own.

Suppliers of Plates

I have been accused of being more interested in the backs of plates than the fronts. But the content of the rectos can usually be seen to better advantage in the form of a print, whereas the versos tell many stories we should not have guessed at even after the most prolonged inspection of a print or the surface from which it was printed.

Many of the surviving copper plates have the name and address of their manufacturer stamped on the back, though the extent of this varies enormously from publisher to publisher. West boasts about the £70 and £80 a year he used to pay his coppersmith "for plates only",[72] and by the greatest stroke of good fortune we can guess the man he is alluding to. The West plate which survives in the Webb collection[73] is marked PONTIFEX | 16 UPPER ST. MARTIN'S LANE. This was a famous firm, trading in the 1790s as Jones and Pontifex at 47 Shoe Lane, then Pontifex alone at 46 and 47, and expanding by the 1830s to become Pontifex, Sons and Wood at 46 and 49, and John Pontifex at 55, with R. Pontifex and Son at 23 Lisle Street, Leicester Square, and (as above) Upper St Martin's Lane.[74]

The firm was patronised by those who could afford the best, such as the amateur naturalists Prideaux Selby and Sir William Jardine, who "both purchased their copper plates and etching ground from Pontifex of London".[75] And thus it comes as no surprise to find West patronising it too.

About 300 of Green's plates survive from the 1830s, when he was still using copper, but although most of them were bought new only seven bear makers' marks: three plates[76] (two from 1834 and one from 1839) having HENRY LARGE | 2 GUNPOWDER ALLEY | SHOE LANE, and four[77] (three from 1836 and one from 1837) having WᴹEASTWOOD | 4 HARP ALLEY | SHOE LANE LONDON. All the rest were presumably bought from other (cheaper?) suppliers, who didn't stamp each plate. William Eastwood was the latest name of a firm founded by Benjamin Whittow (originally Wittau), which occupied various addresses in Shoe Lane from 1763 onwards, eventually moving to Harp Alley c. 1825, the intervening names being Whittow and Large, Whittow and Son, Whittow and Harris, George Harris, and Harris and Eastwood.[78] Henry Large was presumably a descendant of the Thomas Large who was in partnership with Whittow in the 1770s, and there was also a J. Large & Co. in Shoe Lane in the 1830s.

The plates for eight plays by Park survive: four complete or nearly so, and scenes only (no characters) for the other four. All the plates are copper, and all double. Those for the first six plays[79] (c. 1835–40) nearly all bear a maker's mark: W HIAM | 9 RATCLIFFE ROW | BATH Sᵀ | CITY Rᴰ, the only exception being the plates for the fifth play, *The Red Rover*, where the mark is WM HIAM | 9 JOHNS ROW | BATH Sᵀ CITY Rᴰ | LONDON. For the sixth play, *The Wood Daemon*, the address returns to what it was before. (I would guess that, Park, with his very extensive business, kept so many plates ready for use that he sometimes used a new batch before an old one.) The plates of Park's remaining two plays[80] (early 1840s) are almost entirely unmarked, except for one plate[81] which has a figure "4" stamped on the back. Was Park at last drawing in his horns, and going to cheaper suppliers?

Of the few surviving plates by Marks, two bear makers' stamps: one double plate of portraits[82] (1835) came from Eastwood (cf. Green's plates of 1836–37); and a single plate[83] (undated) from Hiam, Ratcliffe Row (cf. the five Park plays of c. 1835–40).

Of the surviving plates by Lazarus (nearly all re-issued by Green), one[84] bears the mark of Eastwood.

Of the various surviving plates by Bishop, one plate of sixes (c. 1840? or later?)[85] bears a maker's mark (the outer lines forming a circle): W LEWIS | 3 ROSE Sᵀ | COVᵀ GARDEN | LONDON.

It is very difficult to generalise about the Skelt plates until the Webb archive is more accessible. Those in private hands seem fairly frequently to have makers' marks: most often Hiam, but also, more interestingly, [crown] | B. WHITTOW [& SONS??] | No. 31 SHOE [LANE] | HOLBORN L[ONDON]. Parts of this mark are missing, because the plate was originally a penny portrait[86] issued c. 1833, and cut down thirty years or so later to make a halfpenny one[87]. Two frontispieces for Skelt playbooks are also reported to have Whittow marks: WHITTOW & SONS | SHOE LANE for *The Waterman* (later 1830s) and B. WHITTOW & SONS for *The Maid and the Magpie* (early 1840s). A brief sketch of the Whittow succession has been given above. It is not clear that the name and address of the plate maker are right for the dates that must be assigned to the engraved plates, so perhaps the plates were part of an old stock, or perhaps (more likely) the Whittow name continued in use at least until the early 1840s. In the Stone Collection two Skelt plates have a Hiam mark.[88] Various Skelt plates in the Baldwin collection also have Hiam marks.[89]

The only Webb plate definitely mentioned as having a maker's mark contains the frontispieces for *Red Riding Hood* and *Richard I* (late 1850s). The mark is W. HIAM.

When Redington began to publish on his own account, he started by getting good copper plates from Hiam. The plate for *Redington's New Orchestra* (one of the last things to be published for him by Green, *c.* 1857) is marked W. HIAM | LONDON, and so are twelve plates of *Paul Clifford*[90] (which I believe to be Redington's first play, *c.* 1858). But the other ten plates of that play are unmarked, and so are the plates of nearly all of Redington's other plays, portraits and miscellaneous sheets (*c.* 1858–64). Presumably he was quicker than Park to realise that Hiam was a bit expensive. The only other marked plates (but their status is ambiguous) are a portrait[91] and a plate of fours[92] (both roughly *c.* 1860). These two plates were made by W^M STILES | [2]3 LISLE STREET | LEICESTER SQUARE | LONDON, but in both cases all of the mark except the word LONDON has been obliterated by a patterned stamp. It is the address which is fascinating, for this is where one of the outposts of the Pontifex empire was once planted. Evidently Redington bought his plates from a supplier who had bought up old stock from a firm which had taken over one of the many premises of West's old coppersmith.

Clearly the making of copper plates was dominated by a group of manufacturers in Shoe Lane and its tributaries, and we should no doubt be finding the same names even if we were investigating another area of printing altogether. A recent book on Spode ware[93] pays particular attention to the makers' marks of surviving plates, and the names of B. Whittow and G. Harris (also John Shafe, London, and John Harlow, Stoke) are frequently found. But it is noticeable that most of the publishers found a local source for their plates, West (Exeter Street, Strand) going to the branch of Pontifex's in Upper St Martin's Lane, while Park (Finsbury), Webb (St Luke's) and Redington (Hoxton) went to Hiam in a street off Bath Street, City Road. Fairburn (Minories and Barbican) also went to Hiam, as did Skelt (Minories). When Marks was at Long Lane (Smithfield) he went to Eastwood in Harp Alley, but when he was at Artillery Lane (Bishopsgate) he went to Hiam. Green (Walworth) may not have had a good local dealer, in which case it would have been natural for him to return to the Shoe Lane fraternity, with which he was no doubt all too familiar from the days when he worked as an apprentice in Denmark Court (Exeter Street, Strand) and lodged in Clement's Inn Passage.

REDINGTON'S NEW DROP SCENE OF THE STANDARD THEATRE.

London, Pub. by J.REDINGTON, 208 Hoxton Old Town, and Sold Wholesale by J.WEBB, 75, Brick Lane, Saint Lukes.

Redington's *Drop Scene of the Standard Theatre* [*c.* 1860], showing aquatinted sky, modern impression (BC)

As we have seen, Green moved permanently from copper to zinc in 1839, so that virtually all his output from the 1840s and 50s is zinc. Of about 600 surviving plates, only two bear suppliers' marks of any kind. One[94] (1846) has a circle with VIVIAN & SON[S?] | SHEET ZINC written round it, enclosing a smaller circle with the figure "17" upside down in the middle. The other[95] (1850) has SOCIETE DE L[A VIELLE-]MONTAGNE surrounding ★★★ | LIEGE | T. The rareness of marked plates among Green's zincs, the use of the expression "sheet zinc", and certain details of the way the plates were cut up, all incline me to believe that Green bought his zinc in sheets and sliced it up himself to create individual plates. Some of these show signs of more than one attempt to make a cut[96], and many of the earliest ones (1840–41) are cut to what is arguably the wrong size: half-an-inch too long[97] or even half-an-inch too big in both directions.[98]

The Swansea firm of Vivian and Sons was founded in 1809 by John Vivian (1750–1826) and his sons John Henry Vivian (1785–1855) and Richard Hussey Vivian, first Baron Vivian (1775–1842). Originally concerned with copper, the firm diversified into zinc smelting and shipping in 1835. This innovation, originally due to J. H. Vivian, was further developed by his son Henry Hussey Vivian, first Baron Swansea (1821–94), who entered the business in 1842. The firm survived until 1924.[99] In the nineteenth century

Top: *Who's best off* ~, inscribed "Rowland-son Invt 1815", discarded, and the back re-used for Green's penny plate of *Top Borders* (1833), printed and coloured by Roger Thompson (BC). *Bottom*: zinc plate, one of three attempts at a label for Thorn's Celebrated Potted Yarmouth Bloaters, the backs re-used for scenes in Green's *Whittington and his Cat* (1853) (DR)

the Belgian town of Liége (since 1946 spelt Liège!) was so thoroughly in-dustrialised as to earn the picturesque sobriquet of "the Birmingham of the Netherlands".[100] Even its priests were industrial chemists, and it was the discoveries of the Abbé Jean-Jacques Dony (1759–1819) which set the region on course for its domination of the zinc market. The company known as *la Société de la Vieille-Montagne* (more fully, *la Société des Mines et Fonderies de Zinc de la Vieille-Montagne*) was founded in 1837 and existed under the same name until 1987. After various amalgamations and incorporations, it is now part of the Umicore group.

Steel plates seem to have been obtained partly from the same suppli-ers as the copper ones, but also from specialists who did not deal in cop-per plates. The surviving steel plates of Fairburn are all from the period 1836–39, and represent four series: a penny series (and "new series") of single portraits, and a penny and halfpenny series of sixes. Most of the sur-viving plates have had their imprint changed to that of W. S. Johnson, only a few retaining the name of Fairburn. I have only been able to examine the altered plates, not the unaltered ones, but I don't think this makes any difference to what follows. A fair proportion of the plates have makers' marks, including the familiar WM HIAM | LONDON on three,[101] N. POWER (up to five times on each plate) on four others,[102] and two difficult-to-read marks together on one plate:[103] [crown?] | PROVAL […] | 18[…] (very large numbers, the "8" not certain) and WINKLES | […1] HAMILTON [ROW?] | [ISL]INGTON | LONDON. Another plate[104] simply has a large D (the same size as the 18 above).

Re-use of Plates

The cheapest way of finding surfaces to print from was to buy up the dis-carded plates of other publishers, or to sort out plates of one's own that were no longer in use, and to engrave on the versos. When Green re-established his business in 1832, he was obviously very strapped for cash, and most of his earliest surviving plates (1833–34) are done on the back of plates bought up from a variety of miscellaneous publishers: a Rowland-son print of 1815,[105] a fashion plate,[106] illustrations from an encylopae-dia,[107] and two little illustrations from *Goldsmith's Geography*, as published by (Sir) Richard Phillips, the associate of Benjamin Tabart.[108] In some cases the plates have been cut down to the required size: thus the title page for somebody's *Three Select Glees and Three Catche[s]*[109] has unfortu-nately had the composer's name chopped off. In others large plates have been cut up to make two or more small ones: thus we can put together two pieces of a garden scene,[110] or some of the component parts of two Dutch views.[111] From 1835 Green was obviously able to buy new plates, though a late example of the re-use of an old one apparently comes in 1849, when a combat was engraved on the back of a view of Holyhead Wake, originally published in 1815.[112] On the other hand, Green did from time to time thriftily engrave things on the back of his own unwanted stock (some of it jobbing printing rather than publications under his own name): a combat taken over from Lazarus,[113] a plate of labels for pickle

Rejected plate 2 of characters from Green's *The Battle of Waterloo* (1842), modern printing from the plate, with plate 1 (same engraver) and plate 2 (substitute engraver) from Pollock's lithographic reprint [1890] (BC, DP)

jars,[114] a rejected plate of characters in *The Battle of Waterloo*,[115] a form for recording casualties,[116] labels or advertisements for Yarmouth bloaters and similar items,[117] the four suits of a pack of small playing cards,[118] a series of comic valentines (21 in all),[119] and a plate of fours in *Dred* published only two years or so earlier by Green's teenage son George.[120] On one occasion only Green had a design engraved on the verso of a plate still in use: *Mary the Maid of the Inn* sc. 6 (1 Jul 1852), using *Jack Sheppard* sc. 8 (26 Dec 1839).

The rejected *Battle of Waterloo* plate helps us to understand something of the relationship between Green and one of the artist-engravers he had been employing for some years, often on plays copied from other publishers (*Aladdin* and *The Maid and the Magpie* from Orlando Hodgson, *The Silver Palace* from Skelt), but also on original work such as *Jack Sheppard*. The last-named play is attributed to William Hornegold, so presumably that is the man we are dealing with. When it came to *The Battle of Waterloo*, he produced the magnificent first plate of characters which is familiar from Pollock's reprint of the play, but then produced a plate 2 which Green thought so unsatisfactory (it is rather on the sketchy side) that he not only rejected the plate, but dismissed the artist, who was not employed by him again for something like a decade. A new plate 2 was commissioned from an engraver who had already produced good work such as the scenes in *The Silver Palace* and the whole of *Harlequin and the Giant Helmet* and was to go on to work for Green right until the latter's death.

Redington never bought up plates for re-use, but he did thriftily re-cycle discarded plates of his own. The characters in some of his early plays (1858–59) are unusually naïve even for the toy theatre, and when he issued

First version of Redington's *The Water-man* [*c.* 1858], printed from the plates by Leonard Petts (BC)

improved versions of *The Mistletoe Bough* and *The Waterman*, some of the old plates were re-used for other things.[121] In 1860, when Redington acquired the major part of Green's stock, he found that had acquired a number of obsolete plates, but that some of the plates for *Blue Beard* (all nine plates of characters, and the first scene) were missing, being now in the possession of Webb, who had acquired a certain quantity of Green's things, albeit tiny in comparison with Redington's haul. Redington had new versions of the missing *Blue Beard* plates prepared, four of which were done on the backs of the obsolete items: a plate of (penny) tricks,[122] *Jonathan Bradford* ch. 4 (also a penny sheet)[123], a (penny?) portrait of *The Duke of Wellington*,[124] and *The Woodman's Hut* ch. 1.[125] The last-named is particularly fascinating, since it is the sole survival of an abortive play of Green's, which perhaps never proceeded beyond this one plate (dated 1 Sep 1842). Like Green, Redington very occasionally resorted to using the back of a plate that was still in use. But he only ever used Green's plates, not his own: *Wreck Ashore* sc. 7[126] and *Lord Darnley* ch. 2 and sc. 6.[127] Pollock only ever had one design engraved on copper, his much-admired plate of *New Policemen*. Having no regular source of supply, he used the back of a portrait by Redington: *Manrico in Il Trovatore*.

As the most famous and successful publisher in the trade, Skelt had a surprisingly frequent recourse to using the backs of old plates. Although he regularly used new plates as well, he used second-hand ones on and off from 1832 to 1843, the entire length of his active play-publishing career. *The Floating Beacon*, one of his earliest pieces, occupies six double plates, all engraved on the back of old caricature plates, usually slightly cut down. At least three are publications by Tegg, 1807–19, including work by Isaac and George Cruikshank and the title page to *The Caricature Magazine Vol. 1*. Moving on a few years, we find two penny plates by Skelt done on the back of two plates by his predecessor and reasonably near neighbour, Frederick Edwards, of Leman Street: namely, the first and last scenes in Edwards's *The Innkeeper's Daughter* (1825).[128] Then there is a sequence of frontispieces done on the back of various old plates (only one likely to have toy theatre connections): "Hodgson's old plate" (but of what I'm not aware),[129] part of a plate entitled *Convicts from the Hulks*,[130] a plate only identified as *Horse Guards*,[131] and part of a plate published from No. 69 St Paul's Church Yard, the long-standing address (1752–1832) of Bowles & Carver, one of the great names in the world of Georgian popular prints.[132]

Re-issuing of Plates

Sometimes publishers bought up the plates of other publishers, and converted them to their own use, altering the name in the heading and (usually) the entire imprint to their own name and address. The most famous example of this is the "Skelt late Lloyd" plates, a much less well-known batch being those taken over from Lazarus by Green. Some of Green's portraits were altered by Redington to new purposes. Among the other surviving plates many portraits by Bishop (1850s??)[133] are taken over from R. Carr (1840s to early 1850s??).[134] Carr, a publisher "not in Speaight", was Bishop's predecessor at 101 Houndsitch, and possibly the same R. Carr who worked in Manchester 1835–43, and printed a version of mummers' play in a chapbook whose mangled text had an effect on almost the entire subsequent tradition of the play and has given folk-bibliographers many a headache.[135]

Alterations to Design

The toy theatre engravers were on the whole very unwilling to make alterations to the design of a plate, once it had been etched. The more confident artists, if they made a hopeless mistake, expected to bluff their way out of difficulties. The most egregious example is in Green's *The Silver Palace*, where the water sprites have shells on their tunics, whereas the villainous fire demons have snakes. Having accidentally given one of the demons a shell, the engraver solves the problem by making snakes emerge from it.[136] But an exception to the general rule was the engraver responsible for the scenes taken over from Lazarus by Green. This man seems

Left: first version of Redington's *The Mistletoe Bough* [*c.* 1859], lithographic print, hand-coloured (BC). *Right*: first version of Redington's *The Mistletoe Bough* [*c.* 1859], modern printing from the plate (BC)

to have been more than usually nervous and indecisive. At least seven of his plates (seven more than most engravers) have fiddly changes made to them.[137] Only one of Green's own scenes has such a change: one of the harlequinade scenes in *Whittington* shows signs that the arch over the fishmonger's first-floor window has been altered, the rather fat end (nearest to the draper's) having originally had a brick passing straight through it.[138] More importantly, Green's view of Redington's shop in *Oliver Cromwell* (Redington had just become his principal agent) was also considerably altered, though this is shown not so much by the plate itself, as by rare "first state" prints taken from it, which show that the "second state" has not only had extra lettering added to Redington's shop (this was easily done), but also the ornate lamp added to the pub next door (this was less easy, and it has been added not in etching but in rather scratchy engraving). I would guess that Redington expected people to use the pub (with its prominent lamp) as a signpost to his own premises, and was annoyed that Green had omitted so essential an ingredient from the scene.[139]

Within Redington's own work, his own view of his shop in *Baron Munchausen* is the only scene to have fiddly alterations. Their purpose is not very clear, but obviously Redington was once again determined to have his premises correctly depicted.[140] The only other Redington plates with changes to the design are plates of stage fronts and orchestras. When orchestras and pediments were split into two, it was evidently the exception rather than the rule, to check whether they fitted together properly before engraving and printing them. Instead, it seems to have been though quite satisfactory to wait until the final printing, discover that the thing didn't work, and then be forced to go back and alter it. Two of the plates are amongst those produced for Redington by Green (both *c.* 1857): *Redington's New Improved Stage Front* (Price Halfpenny) has had the lower top piece altered to match the upper one, and *Redington's New Orchestra* has had the decorative panel under the conductor's stick arm enlarged to match the design under his fiddle arm. The other is Redington's own orchestra (plate unlettered), in which the central portion of the pit (where the two pieces join) is extended, and the size of the three bottom panels is reduced.

Alterations to Lettering

Because calligraphers engraved rather than etched their lettering, alterations to the lettering of a plate were much more easily made than alterations to its design. And they were often necessary, because the calligraphers were often sent information that was illegible, inaccurate, or defective. Often they seem to have been sent an unlettered proof with as much of the required information as the sender had available scribbled on to it. This frequently did not include the serial numbers of portraits, and early impressions with "No. [blank]" are very common. But it was easy to misread numbers: one of the plates of wings in Green's *Dred* was originally issued as no. 48, afterwards corrected to no. 45.[141] (And surviving copies suggest that at least one printing had taken place before the mistake was noticed.) Sometimes mistakes extended over a whole sequence of plates, as when six scenes in Green's *Blue Beard* had to have their numeration corrected.[142] Redington was obviously worried by spelling mistakes, and in *The Miller of Mansfield* one of the plates of characters has had the word "Miller" twice altered (presumably from "Millar", which is possible for a surname but not for an occupation).[143] But Green could be fussy about other things, and the first plate of his *Harlequin and Guy Fawkes* seems to have had the somewhat loose expression "6 Wings" altered to the more precise "6 Pl. Wings".[144]

Detail from plate of characters in Green's *The Silver Palace* (1841), showing shell "corrected" to shell with snakes

The most important type of alteration that could be made to the lettering of a plate occurred when it passed from one publisher to another, so that the name at the top and the imprint at the bottom had to be altered. But it was not easy to do this more than once, and Speaight's observation that "we often find that quite a groove has been worn along the publisher's imprint with the constant changes and erasures" is slightly misleading. A single alteration produced something of a groove (when the plate was attacked from the front and "knocked up" from behind), and if the second imprint needed to be obliterated in its turn, the plate would have stood as much ill-usage as it could take, so that it was safer to add the third imprint in a slightly different position. This explains why Skelt penny plays taken over from Park and Golding have had their headings altered from "Park and Co.'s" to "Skelt's", while those taken over from Lloyd (many of which Lloyd got from Straker) have had their headings expanded to "Skelt's late Lloyd's", further alteration being thought inadvisable.

It is not always easy to interpret the marks on the back of a plate when they suggest that it has been attacked. Sometimes it is possible to conjecture which part of the lettering or design has been altered, but sometimes the "knocking up" seems random. This is especially true with re-used zinc plates. It may be that lumps and bumps on the old verso had to be ironed out before it could become the new recto; but why did the plates have such a consistent allowance of imperfections? Perhaps rather we are

Left: Green's view of Redington's premises (1852), second state, modern printing (DP). *Right*: Redington's own view of his Hoxton premises [c. 1859], reproduced by modern lithography [c. 1945] (DP)

Proof before letters of characters from Park's *Richard the Third* [early 1830s], with the final state of the same plate, after letters and after alteration for re-issue by Skelt [mid-1830s] (BC)

looking at deliberate defacements of an unwanted image, for the benefit of printers who might otherwise have been tempted to print the obsolete side of a double-sided plate.

Scoring through the image would have been simpler, though among the Green and Redington plates this is usually found on a plate taken over from someone else, such as the Rowlandson print mentioned on p. 25 (presumably cancelled before its original owner parted with it). Among the plates of the Webb archive, a few are mentioned as being "scored plates", including sundries issued by Webb from Cloth Fair[145] and miscellaneous scenes, wings and so on by Skelt.[146]

Printing from the Plates

Most conspicuous among the equipment which the toy theatre publishers had to cram into their typically tiny premises was the rolling press, the glorified mangle which squeezed a piece of wet paper into the ink-filled grooves of the engraved plate. Plate-printing may well be the most perverse printing process known to man, only tolerated for so long because it produced work of a delicacy which other methods could not be trusted to achieve. But its labour-intensiveness is almost ludicrous to anyone accustomed to processes where you ink, print, ink, print, with satisfying rapidity. For here you must ink (the whole plate), wipe clean (the surface of the plate but not the grooves), print, and then start the whole business again. It is not the inking which is the killer, but the wiping clean. And whether you are wiping the plates or operating the press, the whole process requires just that combination of brute force and finesse which is particularly wearying. Much pity has traditionally been expended by connoisseurs on those who hand-coloured the sheets (no doubt because they are suspected to have been children), but surely we ought to spare some thought for the printers, who did such hard work so well. And if they sometimes had recourse to getting hopelessly drunk at the end of the week, and keeping a strict observance of "Saint

Proof before stipple and before letters of a sheet of Skelt fours [early 1840s],
with the necessary information added for the calligrapher's benefit (BC)

Monday", who would have the heart to blame them?

At least they got to wear the carpenter's hat, a form of paper hat whose construction is still explained in origami manuals, and whose most famous depiction is in Tenniel's illustration of "The Walrus and the Carpenter", in Lewis Carroll's *Through the Looking Glass* (1872). During the nineteenth century, the hat was worn by stage-hands, known in those days as "stage carpenters", and by a variety of (usually indoor) craftsmen, including printers. Its practical purpose seems to have been to keep bits of paint, ink or glue out of the hair, but it was also something of a badge of office, and West wore his when he sat for his portrait.[147]

Old illustrations of printing establishments always show engravings hung up on strings to dry, in what seems a rather casual and precarious fashion. I have sometimes wondered whether what look like pairs of staple-holes (especially in the prints of Green) do not represent an attempted solution to the problem of hanging up large numbers of wet prints in a small space, particularly since the holes are found in surviving piles of the same design, multiples of which are unlikely to have been stapled together to form a set.

I do not know how the toy theatre publishers stored their plates. Did they use the wooden pigeon-holes like the ones mentioned in note 93? Pollock apparently kept his plates in brown-paper parcels, with the contents carefully detailed on the outside. One of these labels (for the plates of *The Wreck Ashore*) survives with the plates themselves in the Theatre Museum. It lists not only the plates proper to the play (these being the ones contained in the parcel) but also those scenes and wings which are taken from other plays, with instructions where to find them.

Lithography

The toy theatre publishers firmly believed in a hierarchy of techniques, with lithography at the top (too smart for most of their work), engraving in the middle (their usual resort) and woodcut at the bottom (too low for the public they cultivated). This hierarchy is clearly shown by the Twelfth Night characters which Park published in such large numbers. There are two distinct types: the more expensive ones, which have engraved sheets of characters enclosed in a lithographic cover, and the cheaper ones, which have sheets of woodcut characters (with letterpress captions) enclosed in an engraved cover. It will be seen that in each case the wrapping is of a superior quality to the contents, an approach to salesmanship which is still familiar. Nor was this hierarchy only a technical matter for printers: it was recognised by the public too (unconsciously at least, and sometimes consciously).

Although lithography proper was regarded by the toy theatre publishers as something of a luxury medium, it was nevertheless one they were willing to dazzle their customers with from time to time. In 1821 the scene-painter R. Scruton made reproductions of his scenery for *Lodoiska* "Drawn on Stone", and these were sold for him by West, though West was not the actual publisher. The printer is given as "Redman Lithographic Press". The pioneer of lithography within the trade was Park (who had also been the first large-scale producer of halfpenny portraits and of the genre of miniature portraits known as sixes). Having issued both penny and halfpenny portraits in tandem for about a decade, Park

Left: lithographic portrait [1841/42?], perhaps given away with *The Star* magazine (GS). *Right*: lithographic portrait by Park [1844], as tinselled and worshipped by J. B. Howe (PB)

STAR NEW SERIES N°5.   GUNTHORP SC

MISS VINCENT.

AS AGNES PRIMROSE.

Mʳ PHELPS AS HAMLET.

Lithographic portraits by Fortey, who took over the old Catnach Press in 1859: Indian Mutiny and Rifle Volunteers, hand-coloured (GS)

suspended his penny lists at the turn of 1841–42, and shortly afterwards began his new or "Second Series" of penny lithographic portraits, to which was added a series of penny lithographic fours. He may have been influenced by the sort of lithographic portraits of actresses and ballet girls that were starting to be given away with theatrical and other "fast" periodicals at this time.[148] Park's series continued until the mid-1850s, and (suiting impressive subject matter to an impressive medium) concentrated especially on the Shakespearean productions which Samuel Phelps was just beginning to mount at Sadler's Wells. The public was duly impressed. J. B. Howe describes how, in 1844, when he was a boy of twelve, there were published "characters as played by Phelps, done in lithography, which were the first seen in this new style of art, for a penny plain and twopence coloured. There was one which had a special charm for me, on a large scale, which when coloured made a good picture, but when tinselled a better; that was 'Hamlet'. I saved up my pocket-money, bought the tinsel and did it myself, worshipping it for years."[149]

For the time being, there was no rush to follow Park's example, though J. T. Wood (an agent for both Webb and Green) started a lithographic series, which may well be contemporary with Park's.[150] But at the very end of the toy theatre period, from the mid-1850s to about 1863, a number of publishers (some of them the ones we might least expect) produced a small number of lithographic portraits each. Redington produced a large sheet of Fours in *Robert la Grange*, a play of which great things seem to have been expected, but which was not the smash hit people were hoping for. Webb produced two portraits of Garibaldi and two pantomime portraits. Two publishers who went back to grander times, but were now turning towards penny-packet material, make an appearance: Bishop and J. L. Marks. There are also some portraits from Sarah Marks, the widow and successor of J. L. Marks and the eventual owner of Bishop's business too. But the biggest surprise is W. S. Fortey, who had just become the successor to Ryle and Catnach, the chapbook and broadside publishers.[151] The Park family themselves, who had by now suspended their penny series, finally rounded off their halfpenny series with some lithographic portraits, including one of a *Rifle Volunteer* and one of *Garibaldi*. (Since introducing lithography for their penny portraits, they had occasionally slipped a pair of lithographic portraits into the halfpenny series.[152])

The lithographic portraits of this period are part of a general revival of theatrical portraiture. The portraits and miscellaneous other work of Redington are its most conspicuous fruit, to which we may add the portraits of Crawford (he and Redington acted as each other's agent, as Park and Skelt had done a quarter of a century previously), the reproductions by W. S. Johnson of Fairburn's portraits and sixes (sometimes with actors' names altered), the reproductions by Webb of Green's portraits and other work, and the activities of J. K. Green's son George. In addition, some rather grand portraits (on unnecessarily large plates) were issued by an obscure publisher named C. Morrish.[153]

Lithographic Transfer

Though pure lithography is somewhat peripheral to the production of toy theatre prints, from about 1860 onwards printing ceased to be done directly from the copper plates, and was done by lithographic transfer. The pioneer of this method seems to have been Webb, who had been trained in lithography by Park, and who always advertised himself as (among other things) a lithographer. Initially it was as a solution to the problem of stock scenes. One thing that Webb had taken over from Park was the use of double plates, but, although he was always sparing with stock scenes, he presumably didn't want to be in Park's position of not being able to use stock scenes at all, and of having problems even with the use of stock wings. There was also the question of how to present these re-used items to those who bought them. Should Webb (like Green) adopt the bracket system pioneered by Lloyd, or (like Skelt and other publishers) engrave extra information at the sides of scenes when necessary? He did neither, but instead chose (from about 1850) to make lithographic transfers of any scenes he wanted to use as stock ones, substituting the new title during the process of transfer. But for the time being his other work continued to be printed direct from the plates.

In 1855 steam lithography became available, and this was perhaps the catalyst that led to Redington's taking the next step. Although when he branched out on his own (c. 1858) he continued to have nearly all his designs engraved on copper plates, he seems right from the beginning to have had them printed by lithographic transfer. Nor did he print them at home, where, having being trained as a compositor, he only did letter-press printing himself. Instead he sent them out to be printed, apparently in very large quantities. In a great many cases (including nearly all the portraits and miscellaneous sheets), Pollock did not need to print any more copies of Redington's designs than the ones he took over in 1877. Indeed, even as late as the 1950s there were sometimes as many as 500 or 600 copies left of Redington's play-sheets (usually printed 1866–76, but occasionally even earlier). When Pollock took over the business, he reversed Redington's system, toiling all day and night at his lithographic press, and only sending his letterpress work out to other printers.[154]

About 1860 the traditional publishers, under threat from German imports, felt obliged to create theatres with larger scenes. Redington had large scenes designed for a few of his own plays and one or two of Green's, but they were done on copper for lithographic transfer. Webb was now starting to print his ordinary work in this way too. But at some point difficult to ascertain Webb and Park also started producing large scenes for their plays, and these were done in pure lithography. From about 1880 Pollock joined in, having lithographic scenes drawn for him by James Tofts (though they take anything but full advantage of the medium, being the flattest designs that could well be imagined). Webb's large scenes were prettier, but his death in 1890 brought all this creation of new work to an end.

None of the lithographic stones created by Pollock survive. When the

More lithographic portraits by Fortey: the Unification of Italy, hand-coloured (GS)

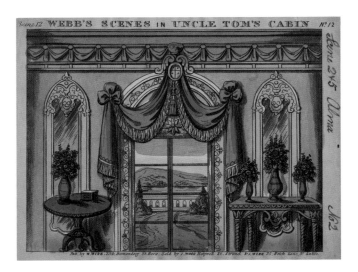
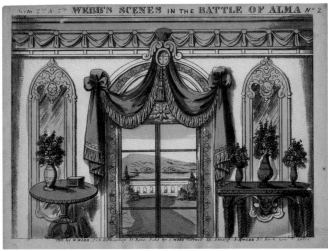

Left: scene originally designed for Webb's *Uncle Tom Cabin* [1853?], printed direct from the plate and hand-coloured. *Right*: the same scene lithographically altered for use in *The Battle of Alma* [1855?], and coloured (DP)

business was bought by Alan Keen, the stones were evidently thought too cumbersome to bother with, and ended up paving someone's garden. The one apparently displayed for several decades at Scala Street was created by William Metcalfe, and was merely a piece of scene-dressing for "Mr Pollock's room", though it fooled almost everyone. It had the Tofts kitchen scene from *The Sleeping Beauty* on one side, and (a bit of a give-away, really) West's print of *Grimaldi's Bang-up* on the other. But in the Webb archive at Princeton there are more than 120 Webb stones, mostly but not all double-sided. A typical size would be 11 x 16 x 2 ¼ inches (or else a surprisingly square 13 x 13 x 2 ¼ inches), and a typical weight 20 lbs, but there seems to be almost no consistency of size at all. The most massive stone is for *Webb's New Stage Front*, 18 x 23 x 3 inches and 112 lbs.

It has always been known that there was a difference between Pollock and Webb as lithographers. Whereas Pollock's lithographic prints come as near to doing justice to their copper and zinc originals as any indirect method reasonably could (they bring out the stipple beautifully, which is a great test), it is difficult not to feel that Webbs the artists were severely let down by Webbs the printers, and the contrast between a good early impression of one of their plates and a blurred lithographic rendering is generally painful. Hitherto no one has been able to guess why this should have been so. But analysis of the content of the surviving stones suggests a reason. Where lithographic transfers were concerned, Webb and Pollock used their stones in very different ways. Pollock used one main stone (large enough for four small plates, or two large), and made his transfers anew for each reprint. But the Webbs seem to have made large numbers of transfers once for all, so that they had to store enormous quantities of stones, not only those with lithographic designs on them (as Pollock also had to do), but dozens with transfers from the copper plates perpetually fixed on them. If these permanent transfers sat about with the ink left to dry on their intricate designs, and at risk of getting scuffed when they were moved or when people barged into them, then it is no wonder that impressions taken from them became increasingly blurred and smudgy.

Lithographic large
panorama from
Park's *The Red
Rover* [*c.* 1870?],
hand-coloured
(BC)

Lithographic large scene drawn on the stone by James Tofts for Pollock's re-issue [early 1880s] of Green's *The Sleeping Beauty* (1850) (DP)

This may not be the whole solution to this problem, but I hope it at least points the way to one.

For many decades collectors have puzzled over the "yellow covers" often supplied with Pollock plays, since they serve no obvious purpose beyond using up images that were originally intended as playbook frontispieces but had become obsolete after such frills had been dispensed with. But the sale of the Robert Scott collection in 2006 brought to light two examples (now in the Alan Powers collection) where we could see these covers being put to their intended use, pasted on to the front of a grey cardboard wrapper for the play in question, with a typeset list of plays, also printed on yellow paper, pasted on to the back. A strange anonymity pervades the whole, with "THE JUVENILE DRAMA" on the

Left: yellow label for *The Daughter of the Regiment*, using the stock surround [1870s] and Green's frontispiece (1857) (BC).
Right: yellow label for Myers & Co.'s *The Juvenile Builder* [1862 or later], on which the Pollock labels were modelled (BC)

familiar front and no name or address on the back. The list of plays suggests the later years of Redington's regime, or the very beginning of Pollock's (roughly, the 1870s). The design of the cover is clearly based on Myers and Co.'s "THE JUVENILE BUILDER", a series of paper toys which in the 1880s Pollock advertised heavily on the wrappers of his playbooks.[155] The spaces following "Plain" and "Colored" are for inserting the price appropriate to the copy in question. Were the yellow covers designed for selling the plays in Oxford Street, with their Hoxton Street origin obscured until the parcel was taken home and unwrapped? Were the "Juvenile Builder" things a good line for Pollock, or was he obliged to plug them to keep Myers sweet? At all events the basic purpose of these mysterious yellow objects is at long last clear.

Lettering for Lithography

It was no doubt for reasons of economy that Redington and the others toy theatre publishers eventually settled for printing by lithographic transfer, but (as Webb early discovered) it did bring some convenience as well. Titles and captions could come and go at will, while imprints and serial numbers could be changed as necessary. In Redington's case, this realisation eventually led to changes in his practice: if addresses and things were only going to need changing, why not leave them blank and fill them in as appropriate? Consequently from many of his later plates he omitted his imprint,[156] or the heading,[157] or both.[158] Sometimes the plate was left with no lettering at all.[159] In most cases the required information was duly transferred to the finished print, though serial numbers were often neglected.

Because there were limits to the frequency with which mistakes in lettering could be altered on a copper plate, it must often have been tempting to give up and hope that no one would notice. But lithography offered opportunities for further precision. The plate for one of Redington's sheets of Fours[160] has a figure of Mr Almar at bottom left, and there was obviously some difficulty in getting the name of his character right. An original wrong form has been corrected to "Sobald", but this is still one letter out, and the correct version, "Lobald" has been added in the margin. On the sheet as printed, the marginal "Lobald" is found lithographically substituted for the name "Sobald" still engraved under the character.

As we have said, Redington in his reprints of Green's sheets favoured what was optimistically known as "artistic" lettering, with curling ascenders and descenders where (in a properly-conducted world) ascenders and descenders perhaps ought not to be. Failing that, he used a very plain and uninteresting variety of stick-lettering. The lettering which thus required to be substituted when Green's plates were transferred to the lithographic stone needed to be stored somewhere, and Redington had one plate that could almost be called a lettering sheet. It began life as a full-size plate, partly occupied by the frontispieces to his *Mistletoe Bough* and *Don Quixote*, but still offering a certain amount of blank space. Redington also used the margins of many of Green's plates as dumping-grounds for

Left: scene in Green's *The Forty Thieves* (1836), in a printing derived from the original plate [*c*. 1945], and as lithographically reprinted, first issued with Redington's "artistic" lettering [*c*. 1870] and then with Pollock's restoration of Green's calligraphy [1880s]. *Right*: plate of characters in Green's *Lord Darnley* (1839), with the same vicissitudes of lettering (DP)

various bits of potentially useful lettering: REDINGTON'S CHARACTERS IN JACK THE GIANT KILLER,[161] TRICKS and the names of six other Green plays,[162] NOTED CHEAP THEATRICAL WAREHOUSE[163], and a placard with "LIST OF PLAYS AND CHARACTERS, &C &C. SEE OTHER SIDE."[164]

Pollock began by continuing Redington's cacographic innovations, but after a short time, in a commendable display of retrotaste, jettisoned these in favour of a return to something like Green's original style of lettering. There were still names and imprints to be altered, and since Pollock, like Redington, did not favour Green's bracket system (lithography and a reduced repertoire of plays made it pointless and even confusing), the scenes had to be given captions. But these were cleverly constructed from bits of Green's own lettering. On Redington's lettering plate, to which

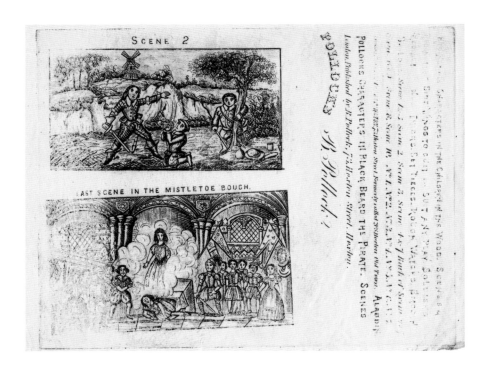

Plate of two Redington frontispieces [*c*. 1859–60], afterwards used as a lettering sheet by Redington and Pollock [1860s to 1880s], modern printing from the plate (BC)

Pollock made additions, is the large ornate POLLOCK'S for use in the cartouche on the first plate of characters of each play. But where is the small POLLOCK'S for use in ordinary headings? It is not to be found on the lettering plate. The clue to the mystery was discovered recently[165] by Hugo Brown while looking over the Edwin Smith printings of Green's plates. One of the character sheets of *Blackbeard the Pirate*[166] (uniquely among hundreds of Green plates) has had GREEN'S altered to POLLOCK'S. Why was it done in that place? Because Pollock wanted it to marry with Green's own headings, and by getting his calligrapher to engrave the word next to a sample of Green's lettering there was a better chance of achieving this than if the word had been engraved in solitary state on the lettering plate. (The sentimentalist in me cannot help noting that, of all the thousand or so plates owned by Pollock, this plate of *Blackbeard* characters must have been the most often held in his hand.)

Webb also needed lettering for his lithographic transfers, and the Webb archive has a number of small lettering plates, some for jobbing printing,

Left: plate of characters in Green's *Blackbeard the Pirate* (1851), with Pollock's name substituted for Green's: print from the zinc plate by Edwin Smith (PTMT).
Right: Pollock's *Characters in Richard the Third* [1880s], originally Green's (1851) (BC)
Below: A portrait intended by Redington to represent *Mr Cooke as Richmond* [c. 1860] somehow acquired the caption *Manrico in Il Trovatore*. *Left*: A Fores impression from the plate [c. 1960] shows the instruction scratched on the plate "Take out Manrico in Trovatore and Put in Richmond" (being written forwards, it prints backwards). *Middle*: A lithographic print [c. 1870] shows the intended result of the change. *Right*: A similar print (with somewhat unusual colouring) shows the real Manrico (BC)

Miss DALY as,
MORGIANNA.
Printed by J. L. Marks, Long Lane Smithfield.

but others for use with theatrical items. One such plate (8¾ x 3½ inches) has WEBB'S FAVORITE CHARACTERS and WEBB'S MILLER AND HIS MEN. Another (8¾ x 2½ inches) has WEBB'S UNCLE TOM CABIN and WEBB'S HUNTER OF THE ALPS and BOB COUSENS PANTALOON and W. HILDYARD CLOWN. A third (3¾ inches square) has "Grindoff" and BOB COUSENS and WALTER HILDYARD and "Figs 3 & 4". Webb's *Uncle Tom's Cabin* included scenes lithographically adapted from his *Forest of Bondy*. So did *The Miller and his Men*, and one of its scenes had an added figure of "Grindoff". *The Hunter of the Alps* was a late production (planned early 1860s, but not executed till 1880), and so involved more lithographic work than earlier pieces. The other inscriptions are for Webb's two sheets of fours adapted from Fairburn/Johnson sixes (date uncertain) and for his two lithographic pantomime portraits (1863). The version of these inscriptions transcribed from the long plate is the one actually used on the portraits (which likewise lack the expected "as"). What the version on the square plate was intended for is not clear. Perhaps it is a rejected first attempt. (W. Hildyard was indeed Walter, often known as "Wattie".) I am not sure what "Figs 3 & 4" is intended for.

Woodcuts

Woodcutting was very largely shunned by the toy theatre publishers, who (despite the new school of wood engraving pioneered by Bewick) perhaps still associated woodcuts with Catnach and the Seven Dials. Woodcut theatrical portraits were in fact produced by Catnach's great rival Pitts *c.* 1820, but they are very rare and not always attractive. I remember one in the Brady Collection (*Mrs Egerton, as Helen Macgregor*) that I couldn't wait to get back in its envelope; on the other hand, one of a Fury in *Don Giovanni* (which David Drummond exhibited in his window a few years ago)

Top: woodcut portrait, with typeset border and lettering, published by J. L. Marks [1840s?]. *Below*: characters (woodcut) and playbook (with crude colour lithography) issued by *The Boys of England* magazine [*c.* 1870] (BC)

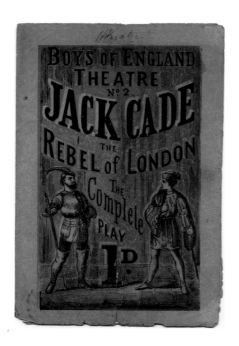

seemed rather impressive. Pitts evidently thought so too, as the figure was later used at the top of a long song-sheet.[167] No theatrical portraits by Catnach himself have ever been spotted, while his ultimate successor Fortey surprisingly went in for lithographic portraits, as we have seen. Somewhat of the Pitts school are some characters in *The Miller and his Men* by J. Quick, whom A. E. Wilson has taught generations of toy theatre enthusiasts to regard as "nearly the worst of any publisher".[168] This is not necessarily unfair, but it is unfortunate, as the Quicks were a distinguished family of wood-engravers, who often produced brilliant work, and continued to practice well into the twentieth century, when they were patronised by such giants of fine printing as the Nonesuch Press and the Society of SS. Peter and Paul.

Among the mainstream toy theatre publishers, the only one to make

Left: characters from an anonymous penny-packet version (woodcut) of *Black-Eyed Susan* (BC). *Right*: Speed to Clarke's, of Garrick Street! a penny packet publisher in the West End: detail from the sheet reproduced overleaf (BC)

A sheet by Andrews (derived from one by Skelt late Lloyd late Straker), with type-set lettering superimposed (BC)

Penny packet harlequinade (woodcut, hand-coloured), published by H. G. Clarke (BC)

much use of woodcut was J. L. Marks, who, probably in the early 1840s, produced a nice series of woodcut portraits. These appear in two forms: one with typeset borders and Marks's imprint; the other, printed on smaller paper, with no borders and no indication of publisher. Other publishers made use of woodcut for their cheaper sundries (valentines or Twelfth Night characters and so on), but not for their theatrical work, and not even for their specially-adapted playbooks, which in the "halfpenny" period invariably had engraved frontispieces, even though respectable acting editions (such as Cumberland's, available from the 1820s onwards) would have given an obvious precedent for a text "embellished with a fine wood-engraving". At the very end of his career Green started issuing his playbooks with a wood-engraved design on the cover (morticed in two places for insertion of typeset title and serial number), but this choice of medium seems to have been forced on him as a last resort. The woodblock does not survive, but an earlier version of the design, etched on a zinc plate, is in the Robinson collection, and prints taken from it by Edwin Smith suggest that the etched version was a failure. It is likewise morticed for insertions (to be written in by hand, as was surprisingly common at this period?), but this is not practicable in plate-printing. The holes in the plate bring up unsightly blisters in the paper, and cheap paper would surely tear at these points. Nor does the rest of the etched design seem to print very clearly. Hence the resort to a wood-engraved substitute.

But it was left to the boys' magazines (1865 and onward) and the "penny packet" publishers (same period?) to make really significant use of woodblock printing. And both types of publisher were simply extending their usual methods, the magazines taking the empire-building style of wood-engraving which illustrated the adventures of their boy heroes, and applying it to their toy theatre plays (which included dramatised versions of the same stories, along with *The Miller and his Men* and other more traditional fare), while the penny packets took the cruder, more vigorous (but often well-drawn and thoroughly humorous) styles of wood-cutting familiar from their shadow shows and paper toys, and applied them to illustrating a range of (mainly traditional) toy theatre plays. As far as I know, no woodblocks relevant to the toy theatre survive. Blocks for some shadow-theatre figures of the "penny packet" type were certainly owned by Gerald Morice, but most of them are no longer in the Morice Collection.

The penny packet publishers more often produced original work than they are given credit for, but they did also issue work that was simply copied from the old plays of Skelt and others. Mathews (some of whose work was in "penny packet" form, and who from a printing point of view fits in most easily with this group) made close re-drawings of the sheets he wanted to copy, and his drawings were turned into metal reliefs (copper? or copper alloy?) for printing. A few of these survive in the Baldwin collection, still pinned on to blocks of wood. Andrews, who had the most extensive repertoire of the pure "penny packet" publishers, did not bother with re-drawing, but seems to have had printing plates made direct from old prints. He may have had the old copper plates to work from in some cases, since his repertoire is notable for the number of plays in it whose plates were NOT owned by Webb, but there were certainly some cases (such as *Tom Tucker*) where Andrews was able to issue a play even when the plates WERE owned by Webb. But by this time working from prints

Block for the top half of a plate of characters in Mathews' *Jack O'Newbery* [1890s?], re-drawn from Green's *State Secrets* (1837), with the whole plate as printed (PB).

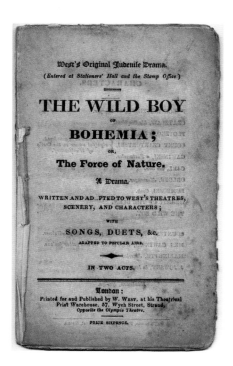

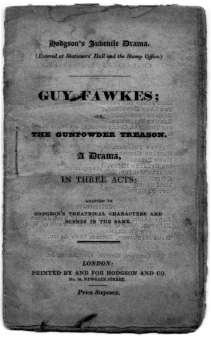

Top: playbook for West's *The Wild Boy of Bohemia* (1827), "Printed by R. Thomas, Denmark Court, Strand" (PB). *Bottom*: playbook for Hodgson and Co.'s *Guy Fawkes* (1822) (PB)

was quite possible. A cheap publisher such as Dicks, for instance, managed to issue during the 1880s versions of the novels of Dickens and his contemporaries in which the original illustrations of Phiz and Cruikshank were very well reproduced (better than in many modern editions), yet he did not possess any of the plates.

Letterpress

Although they were obliged to keep a rolling press (and sometimes as many as three)[169] on their premises, some of the toy theatre publishers managed without a common press, and sent their letterpress work out. Certainly many of them failed to register a common press, at a time when this was a legal requirement (1799 onwards), so that, among publishers mainly concerned with the toy theatre, only Lloyd, Skelt and Park seem to have registered their presses (1831, 1835 and 1837 respectively, in each case several years after the start of the business).[170] In 1811, when West wanted to issue a catalogue of his prints, he did it in the form an elaborate engraved sheet, partly no doubt because this was the only way he could do it under his own steam. In the late 1820s, when he rather belatedly started to have playbooks printed to go with his characters and scenes, he sent them out to one or other of the legion of printers operating in his immediate vicinity. (He hardly ever used the same printer twice, so perhaps he was always on the look-out for somebody cheaper.) In the 1830s and 40s, he claimed to be the printer of the pornographic songsters he issued, but as falsity of imprint is the norm in clandestine works, the implication that he had finally acquired a common press is not as certain as might first appear. (He might simply have been avoiding owning up to being the publisher.) Hodgson and Co., who were the pioneers of toy theatre playbooks in the early 1820s, had some of their later books printed by G. H. Davidson, stereotype printer. Davidson eventually became a notable publisher of cheap music, and the proprietor of Cumberland's acting edition of plays.

By the halfpenny period, most of the publishers were claiming to be the printers of their own books. In the case of Green, the obvious inadequacy of his equipment forbids us to doubt this; with Skelt and Park, the subterranean standards of their grammar and spelling perhaps point to a similar conclusion. Webb is better on both counts; but the most literate and well-printed books (however surprising this may seem) are Redington's. Like Webb, he was a member of a better-educated generation than the others, but he was also a trained compositor. By the time we get to Pollock, although the playbooks claim to be printed by him, this seems to be more a matter of pride than veracity. He is known to have sent his books out, and their differing styles of printing show that the world around him was changing. See especially *The Battle of Waterloo* and *The Sleeping Beauty*, which have all the vulgarity and messiness of modern commercial printing.

Because the presses owned by the toy theatre publishers were often small, they had to make the best use of them by resorting to what now

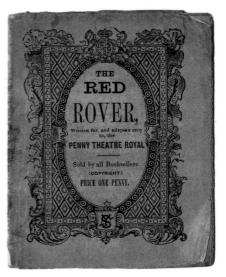

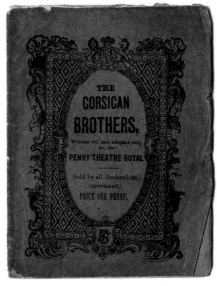

seem rather strange formats. The books of both Webb and Green, for instance, tend to consist of a half-sheet of 18mo. The disadvantage of this 3 x 3 arrangement is that it cannot be folded in such a way as to allow sewing along the spine; it has to be stabbed.

Paper and Watermarks

The paper used by the toy theatre publishers certainly varied in quality. West sometimes used very beautiful paper, and sometimes rather curious paper, such as the blue-ish paper he favoured in the late 1820s and early 30s. But, just as with the designs, the contrast between the wonderfulness of West and the awfulness of everybody else can be (and has been) overdone. The paper the halfpenny publishers used served its turn pretty well, and by the later period of Webb and Pollock one can only marvel that both firms managed to obtain supplies of paper for their lithographic printing that were so consistent in size and quality over a period of seventy years or more. In the twentieth century the fluctuations of paper quality are one of the great aids to spotting what printers have actually been getting up to. They help us to distinguish between the many types of direct and indirect reprint undertaken both on the Webb and Pollock fronts, as well as by private individuals and (though this has been very rare) by what one might go so far as to call forgers. The best-known series of forgeries contains portraits of actors in roles which perhaps should have been commemorated in theatrical portraits of the twopence coloured kind but unfortunately never were. One (Mr Kean as Lear, supposedly by Hodgson and Co.) was reproduced in a book of 1946,[171] and the zinc plate for another (Mr Kean as Hamlet, supposedly by Dyer) is in the Gerald Morice Collection.

Between 1944 and 1968 both the Keen and Fawdry regimes made an

Above: playbook, with folding hand-coloured frontispiece, for Orlando Hodgson's *The Miller and his Men* (1832): "Sears & Trapp, Printers, 11, Bridge Row, Walbrook" (PB). *Left*: three little playbooks by the penny packet publisher Yates and Co., of Nottingham (PB)

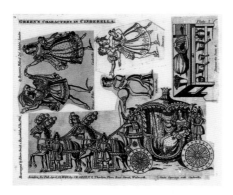

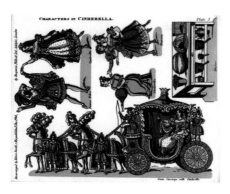

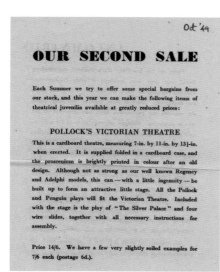

attempt to keep up the stocks of the old Pollock repertoire. Indeed, one of Keen's first acts was to commission reprints of the scores of sheets that were by now out of print. These were done on very thin paper, no doubt all that was available at the very end of the War. The sheets were printed by modern lithography, but derived their images direct from the copper plates, so that the old Pollock sheets were now mixed up with Greens, Redingtons and Parks, as the case might be. (In fact, they had always been mixed up with Redingtons.) Mrs Fawdry also reprinted a small number of sheets, but her reprints were on rather thick paper, and derived sometimes from the old prints, and sometimes from the plates, depending on what came to hand. In 1960 *Richard the Third* was reprinted in book form, and that arrangement has remained the norm for facsimile reprints ever since.

The study of watermarks in toy theatre printing has hardly begun in earnest. A start was made by Desmond Seaton-Reid, who in his West catalogue reports a number of dated watermarks on West prints. But these are not usually very exciting, being typically a year or two before the date of the plate (original printing, then) or a few years later (early reprint). No one has yet unearthed the sort of spectacular discrepancies to be found in other areas of inquiry, such as turn-ups, where those published by Sayer in the 1770s frequently turn up at auction on paper watermarked 1818 (or thereabouts). To children of the 1820s the fashions of fifty years earlier must have seemed hopelessly quaint and old-fashioned, yet still someone thought it worthwhile to re-issue these old things. So far, the only discovery of this magnitude among toy theatre prints involves West's three sheets of proscenium ornaments (1829), once part of the Webb collection and now owned by David Robinson. Plate 1 is watermarked J WHATMAN 1853, the year before West's death. Was he reprinting things right up till the end? Were the prints made specifically for inclusion in the sale of his effects in 1855, before the plates were broken up? Or did someone manage to acquire the plates, so that they were able to print from them? (But although the Webbs owned multiple copies of the prints, there is no direct evidence that they ever owned the plates.)

Modern Methods

Apart from the occasional introduction of electric lighting to the wooden stages (for which there is some evidence in the earlier twentieth century), the application of modern methods to the production and operation of toy theatres was very largely the work of Alan Keen and his co-adjutors Edwin Smith and George Speaight. These methods included colour printing, cardboard theatres, simplified versions of child-friendly titles,

Top: red, yellow and blue separations (without the black outlines) on a sheet of characters in Green's *The Silver Palace* (1841), for lithographic colour-printing (1946) (BC). *Middle*: detail of Edwin Smith preparations for a sheet of characters in Green's *Cinderella* (1849), with the colour-printed result (1947). *Bottom*: typically stylish advertisement for a sale by the sinking Keen regime (1949) (BC)

Label for a packet of printed copies of a G. Skelt sheet [*c.* 1950], secured with tape bearing the name and address of the Shirley Press, Southampton (BC)

Below: William Metcalfe. *Bottom*: Richard Metcalfe

the issuing of "kits" (theatre, play, and various accessories), lighting sets involving torch bulbs and batteries, and mass-production generally. They bought no immediate commercial success, but they pointed the way of the future with a sure sense of direction.

The stylishness of Keen's printing (including his enthusiastic advertising) owed much to his employment of the Favil Press, a firm whose origins were interwoven with those of the Cayme Press, one of the more curious private presses of the 1920s. The Favil Press was dedicated to producing stylish work at a reasonable cost, and was known for such good works as printing the daily programmes for the concerts given during the war in the denuded National Gallery.

Between the end of the war and his death in 1956, George Connetta ("G. Skelt") of Jersey produced an enormous quantity of lithographic reproductions of the old toy theatre sheets of Skelt and others. These were printed for him, rather forcefully but on paper of excellent quality, by the Shirley Press, Southampton. Marguerite Fawdry, who bought Connetta's stock of printed sheets after his death, wrote to the printers in 1958 to inquire about the plates from which the designs had been reprinted, but they had already been destroyed. Collectors of these reprints have often been puzzled by the mixture of two types of reproduction, often within the same play: some plates being photographed directly from the old sheets, others being done indirectly from Connetta's spidery re-drawings. I suspect that the explanation is a very simple and practical one: where he had plain copies of the old sheets, he had them reproduced directly; where he only had coloured copies, he made tracings from them in order to create a plain version for reproduction. A few of his tracings are in the

Left: Green's penny portrait *Mr Yates as Red Rover* (1842), printed by David Powell and coloured by Leo Pimlott (1984) (BC). *Middle*: Redington's portrait of *Mr C. Pitt as Charly Wag* [*c.* 1861], altered from a portrait by Green of a character in *Dred* [*c.* 1857], impression from the plate by Roger Thompson, with his colouring [1978–80] (BC). *Right*: the same portrait, impression from the plate by Fores of Bond Street (BC)

Redington portrait *Mr Phelps as Falstaff*, impression from the plate by Fores [*c.* 1960], with colouring possibly by "Grandpa" Fawdry (BC)

Brady Collection, Christ Church, as are some proof sheets of otherwise unknown publications.

Keen had the Favil Press, and Mrs Fawdry had the Soho Press, Wardour Street, which was founded by the brothers William and Harold Metcalfe, and was originally the printing arm of Paxton and Co., music publishers, though allowed to take in outside work when time permitted. Of the long service given to Pollock's by William Metcalfe and his son Richard, it is hardly possible to speak with sufficient gratitude. Nothing was ever too much trouble for them in preparing work for printing, and their standards of craftsmanship were always impeccable. In such practical matters as payment and storage they were always more helpful than anyone could reasonably have expected. And their resourcefulness never gave out. When the series of facsimile reprints organized by Barry Clarke and underwritten (all but one) by John Holt was first projected, Richard showed how the introduction of computer printing (new to Pollock's) could help to achieve the desired ends at a reasonable cost.

One of the stranger inheritances linking the Keen and Fawdry periods is the use of colour separations, a process which evidently had cheapness to recommend it but certainly not convenience. In effect, the colourist has to apply each of the constituent four or five colours to a blank gelatine without being able to see the overall effect. I have known people deny that such a method was known to printing, but it was certainly used at Pollock's from the 1940s to the 1970s. One of the last experts in its use was Robert Culff, who applied it to his 1965 abridgement of *The Children in the Wood*. But he showed no willingness to pass on the mysteries to a new generation, and when Roger Thompson was having difficulty preparing *The Corsican Brothers* (1974), an appeal was made to his predecessor on his behalf. "Roger has started it, Roger can bloody well finish it," snapped Culff, disappearing in the direction of Spain, his last abode. But Thompson, if obliged to be self-taught, nevertheless finished his work with great gusto. One blemish (the face of Doctor Tardieu has been left white) only serves to illustrate the difficulties that have to be overcome in this fiendishly difficult method of colouring.

In the years running up to 2004, stocks of cardboard theatres had declined dangerously, but the uncertainties of the time made it impossible to commission reprints. The problem was solved by Horatio Blood, who adapted the theatres to sizes that could be reproduced by colour photocopying. His ingenuity in this regard puts him firmly in the line leading back through Peter Jackson and Peter Adams Turner to the great Edwin Smith.

Perhaps the only person in recent decades to publish plays and portraits without any concession to modern methods has been Joseph Hope-Williams. His productions are engraved on and printed from copper plates, and coloured in the traditional manner. Their complete authenticity has sometimes been a snare for the unwary, and I have seen a museum web site in which it is claimed that *Maria Marten; or, The Red Barn* was made into a nineteenth-century toy theatre play, on the strength of *Hope's Characters and Scenes* in the same.

The Old Methods kept Alive

Unlike the house of Redington-Pollock, which, once they had gone over to lithographic transfer, never printed directly from the plates (not even to oblige a customer, as far as I know), the Webbs continued to keep both methods going, satisfying small demands by direct printing, and using lithography where they hoped the demand would be greater. They were thus well placed to be the pioneers of printing for a collectors' market. And by the 1920s it seems clear that H. J. Webb was using copperplate printing to fill gaps in his own plays;[172] to reprint for collectors the plays of Skelt for which he held plates; and to reprint the Fairburn/Johnson portraits, which formed such an excellent basis for the many tinsel portraits he created.

There was none of this at Pollock's until the Keen regime, which oddly chose to print 25 copies of Green's *Therese* for general sale, as well as allowing Edwin Smith to reprint all sorts of things, partly as a basis for his colour adaptations, and partly for his own amusement. In addition, other reprints were made, very nicely done, though on thin paper, which crinkled under the stresses of printing. These notably include two Newgate dramas (*Jack Sheppard* and *Sixteen String Jack*), presumably at the request of someone keen on highwaymen. (Were they done in order to inspire J. B. Priestley and Doris Zinkeisen to create their new juvenile drama *The High Toby*, in 1947?)

Between the late 1950s and about 1970, large numbers of the Pollock plates were sent to Fores of Bond Street to be printed. In previous writings I have wondered about the exact numbers that were printed, but I

Top: Redington portrait *Mr Holloway as Richard the 3rd*. *Middle*: Redington portrait *Mr Anderson as Macbeth*. *Bottom*: Redington's pantomime fours [*c.* 1860]: impressions from the plates by Roger Thompson [*c.* 1978], with his colouring (BC)

59

now realise that this is an artificial question. Orders were solicited in advance, and the printing was done on that basis, though Mrs Fawdry had additional copies printed and coloured for herself, including a set of Green's *Rob Roy* coloured by Martin Roland[173] in such a happy imitation of Lucy Adlam's style as to make one forget momentarily that this was a play Miss Adlam never had the opportunity of colouring.[174]

Other plates were printed in house, some of the best early printings (there were some very rough ones produced as well) being by Leonard Petts, a name well known to aficionados of old gramophone records. In the 1970s Roger Thompson both printed and coloured plates in fine style. In the 1980s the present writer (having been given expert instruction by Debby Brown) did a certain amount of printing, though, as he had no skill with a brush, his efforts were coloured for him by Leo Pimlott.

As in so many areas, a little experience only increases one's admiration for the old practitioners. Though the old "halfpenny" prints have their weaknesses (unevenness of inking, outer areas of the plate not properly inked, little blobs of ink left on the edge of the plate), these are easily forgivable when we think of the furious pace at which the old printers must have worked. But most modern pulls (even those emanating from Bond Street) suffer from an inability to get the surface of the plate completely free of ink. A thin film always remains. There are various ways of disguising this (see the Fores plates again, which are very ingenious in this respect), but apparently none of solving it. Yet the old printers, even working under the pressure that they did, got the surfaces of their plates amazingly clean. What was their secret?

1. George Speaight, *Juvenile Drama* (1946), in which the chapter on printing is still a must for anyone who wants to know the basics of the thing. I cannot hope to match its mixture of accuracy, concision and reader-friendliness, and I have not tried to do so

2. Or, strictly, owned by Kenneth Fawdry, who when his wife was struggling to establish her business in its early days, supplied her with capital by buying the plates from her for £50. I was told this story by the two people involved, but I seem to be the only living soul who now remembers it

3. Despite being technically etchings, the prints are usually referred to as engravings, and their executants as engravers. And although, as we shall discuss below, other materials than copper eventually came into use, contemporary usage sometimes at least referred to "copper-plates", even when other types of metal plate were included (see p. 23)

4. Gerald Morice and George Speaight, "New Light on the Juvenile Drama", in *Theatre Notebook*, xxxvi (1971–72), pp. 115–121. This consists of a reprint of Henry Mayhew, "Letter XXXVIII – 25 February 1850" [= Mayhew interview 1850/1972], with a brief introduction and commentary. At one point West categorically states "I found the copper." He also refers to an artist who did work "unbeknown to me on a copper of mine" (both at p. 118)

5. Ralph Thomas, conversation with George Cruikshank, quoted in George Speaight, *The History of the English Toy Theatre* (revised edition 1969) [= Speaight], p. 71

6. Mayhew interview 1850/1972, p. 120

7. Mayhew interview 1850/1972, p. 120

8. Those bought by Speaight have now been acquired by Peter Baldwin; some of those bought by Morice passed to Robert Scott, and these too are now in the Baldwin collection

9. For more on the Webb archive, see David Powell, *W. G. Webb and the Victorian Toy Theatre* (2005), especially the Appendix, pp. 35–36

10. I have discussed the *Wapping Old Stairs* drawings in my Historical Note to the "Holt" reprint of *The Silver Palace*: they are very lightly and neatly drawn, but laid out as if for penny rather than halfpenny sheets, thus leading to the rather squashed effect of the resulting prints

11. The Ralph Thomas Collection, British Museum (Print Room), bought 1886

12. Letter from E. L. Pollock (Benjamin's daughter Louisa) to George Speaight, 20 Nov 1940. Miss Pollock mentions *Richard the Third* ch. 3, 4, 8, 9, and sc. 1, but not sc. 9, though this was certainly missing by a few years later

13. *The Sleeping Beauty* sc. 4, 7, 10, 11

14. *Baron Munchausen* sc. 8

15. The Sage Collection of Juvenile Drama is at Victoria University, British Columbia, Canada

16. Portrait no. 44 *Mons. Louis as Clown*, portrait no. [45?] *Mr. G. French as Harlequin*, portrait no. 46 *Madame Auriol as Columbine*

17. *Redington's Drop Scene of the Surrey Theatre* no. 4

18. *The Miller and his Men* ch. 1–4; *The Children in the Wood* ch. 1–3, sc. 3 (the only non-stock scene in the play)

19. *The Life of a Soldier* ch. 5–8, sc. 1, 3, 10, 11, wg 37 (all the non-stock scenes and wings), and sc. 7 (stock)

20. *Mr. Wightman as Richard III* [original date unknown], re-issued by Webb as portrait no. 29 *Mr. Rickards as Richard III* [later 1850s]

21. A library, the benefaction of Lloyd E. Cotsen, within the Department of Rare Books and Special Collections, Princeton University Library

22. *The Blood Red Knight, Rob Roy, Ivanhoe, Mary the Maid of the Inn, The Wandering Boys*, and two plays unidentified

23. *Blue Beard*

24. *Aladdin* and *The Maid and the Magpie*

25. *Red Rover*

26. *Richard Turpin*

27. *The Silver Palace, The Miller's Maid, The Woodman's Hut, The Blind Boy, The Forty Thieves, Harlequin and Old Dame Trot, Harlequin Little Tom Tucker, The Waterman, Robinson Crusoe, The Brigand, Othello, Pizarro, The Wood Daemon, Der Freischutz*

28. *Mazeppa*

29. *New Demons* nos 1 and 2 (re-published by Webb 3 Nov 1879)

30. *Richard the Third* ch. 8, 9 (but not currently ch. 3, 4, sc. 1, 9). How and when King acquired these plates, I am puzzled to explain

31. Halfpenny portraits nos 71/72, halfpenny combats nos 11/12; penny sixes no. 14

32. Portrait no. 50, fours no. 2 (of Kean), sixes no. 1 new series

33. Portrait no. 11, portrait of Van Amburgh no. 26 (what series?), combat no. 3

34. See note 17

35. Sixes no. 2 (of Master Burke)

36. *Mr Lewis as Timurkhan in the Orphan of China* (8 May 1826)

37. *Collector's Miscellany*, December 1936

38. There are many blocks in Morice Box 153 and Box 154, but they are mostly modern, and connected with Morice's own writings. Two of his shadow blocks (one by G. Ingram, and one by Goode Bros.) were reproduced in *The Puppet Master* vol. 7 no. 3 (Spring 1963). Others now missing include one of nursery-rhyme figures and "the key-block for a 'Proscenium', complete with orchestra strip at one side"

39. *Victoriana and Collectors' Items*, 23 April 1996, lots 271 and 272, "A collection of approx. 30 copper Plates, for theatrical prints, mainly by Skelt, nearly all of multiple subjects" and "A similar lot" respectively

40. Penny sixes no. 4 [early 1830s, re-issued *c.* 1834]

41. *Hodgson's New Foot Peices* [*sic*] *Descending Car's* [*sic*] *&c. No. 4* (1823), a large threepenny sheet signed by George Childs

42. No. 25 *Mr. Fillingham as Tom King* (7 Jun 1841)

43. No. 24 *Mr. S. Foster as Dick Turpin* (24 May 1841)

44. *Mr Cobham as Arbaces – Mr Freer as Glaucus* [obviously *The Last Days of Pompeii*] [*c.* 1834, signed "E Lazarus Fec."], the verso used for Green's *Wapping Old Stairs* sc. 7 (1 Feb 1838)

45. *Mr Palmer as Ahasuerus in The Triumph of the Jewish Queen* [*c.* 1835, re-issued by Green 20 Mar 1837]

46. *The Wreck Ashore*, including wg 18, 19 and many scenes subsequently used as stock ones [*c.* 1835, re-issued by Green 1 Jun 1837]

47. Green's *State Secrets* sc. 3 (1 Mar 1837), *The Lord Mayor's Fool* sc. 3 (1 Apr 1837), to which others could easily be added on stylistic grounds, but a number of plates for these plays are missing, so the final confirmation remains to be made

48. I quote this from my memory of looking over the Webb drawings at the Sotheby's sale in 1994. I fear my version is not verbatim, but I hope it conveys the authentic flavour of deliberate slanginess. Suzman had been asked to give a portrait more background, and this is his commentary on the result

49. [David Powell,] *William West & the Regency Toy Theatre* (2004) [= West catalogue], p. 28, no. 4

50. Penny sixes no. 14 (Stone Collection), *Skelt's Horse and Foot Band* no. 3 (Baldwin collection)

51. No. 8 in Skelt's penny series [*c.* 1834], having perhaps been no. 3 in Straker's original series [1828]

52. For instance, *Skelt's Horse and Foot Band*, as in n. 50

53. See notes 31 and 32

54. No. 18 in Skelt's penny series [*c.* 1834], having perhaps been no. 13 in Straker's original series [1829]. The plate is framed, so it is impossible to check for the tell-tale signs of alteration and re-alteration

55. A. E. Wilson, *Penny Plain Two Pence Coloured* (1932) [= Wilson], p. 56

56. Penny portraits no. [2?] and [3?] *Mr Diddear as King Arthur* and *Mr T. P. Cooke as Sir Roland* [*c.* 1835], re-issued as halfpenny portraits no. 48 and 49 (1 Jun and 1 Jul 1849) respectively, and further re-issued by Webb as portraits no. 35 and 34 [*c.* 1860] respectively, the plates being now in the Robinson collection. The title of the portrait of Cooke has been shifted by Green from the bottom to the top of the plate, in order to fit the smaller size of paper

57. See p. 34

58. Most notably, penny portraits no. 9 *Mr. Yates as the Red Rover* (16 Aug 1842) and no. 12 *Mr. Braham as Tom Tug* (1 Dec 1842)

59. For details of two such plates, see pp. 29–30, with notes 86 and 87

60. Speaight, p. 58

61. Unfortunately the Judd lists of the Webb archive, which contain so much minute detail about the collection, even to giving the weight of the plates and the lithographic stones, are usually silent about the material of the plates, though they do sometimes mention it; and similarly makers' marks, though transcribed in some parts of the list, are probably not always recorded. But Laurie Webb thinks that silence always means copper

62. See previous note

63. *Mr. E. F. Saville as Barnard Jasper* and *Mr. Dale as Claude Amboine* (Feb 27 and Mar 20 1843)

64. *Mr. N. T. Hicks as Richard 1st* (Jan 15 1844)

65. *The Forest of Bondy* [1847] and *Union Jack* [1848]

66. *The Duke of Cambridge* and *Napoleon III, Emperor of the French*; *The Emperor of Russia* and *The Sultan of Turkey*; and *Admiral Dundas of the Black Sea Fleet* and *Sir Charles Napier Admiral of the Baltic Fleet* [mid-1850s]

67. *Webb's Miniatures* nos 1/2 and 3/4 [1850s?]

68. Ch. 1-8 and sc. 1/2 on steel; sc. 5/6 and ch. 9/sc. 11 on copper; sc. 7/8 and 9/10 on the back of old copper plates by F. Edwards (1825-26); set pieces, water pieces and wings on plates of unknown material

69. Wilson, p. 53

70. Penny portrait no. 111 *Master Owen, as Young Norval* (3 Dec 1838) and halfpenny portrait no. 150 *Master Owen as Young Norval* [*c.* 1840]

71. For much of this paragraph, I am indebted to the recent researches of Horatio Blood, who has quite revolutionised my thoughts on the subject

72. Mayhew interview 1850/1972, p. 120

73. *Mr. Wightman as Richard III* [original date unknown], re-issued by Webb as portrait no. 29 *Mr. Rickards as Richard III* [later 1850s]

74. Ian Maxted, *The London Book Trades 1775–1800: a Preliminary Checklist of Members* (1977) [= Maxted], *s.vv.* Pontifex, William; Jones and Pontifex

75. Christine E. Jackson, *Bird Etchings: The Illustrators and their Books, 1655–1855* (1985), p. 202

76. *Douglas* ch. 2, 3 (1 Nov 1834) and *Lord Darnley* ch. 5 (1 Apr 1839)

77. *Robert Macaire* sc. 2 (15 Feb 1836), *The Forty Thieves* ch. 8, 9 (1 Apr 1836) and *Blue Beard* ch. 1 (1 Dec 1837)

78. Maxted, *s.vv.* Whittow, Benjamin; Whittow and Large; Large, Thomas

79. *The Old Oak Chest, The Miller and his Men, The Woodman's Hut, The Blind Boy, The Red Rover, The Wood Daemon*, none dated but the order made clear by the wing numbers

80. *Der Freischutz, The Maid and the Magpie*

81. *Der Freischutz* sc. 1/2

82. *St George & the Dragon* and *St Patrick & the Griffin* (14 Oct 1835)

83. *Mr. Kean as Rolla* (undated, but from Marks's "2nd Series")

84. *The Wreck Ashore* (Lazarus [*c.* 1835?], re-issued by Green 1 Jun 1837)

85. Brian de Bois Guilbert, etc. (undated, but a companion plate is a copy of a Park plate of sixes, which probably dates from the late 1830s)

86. Penny portrait no. 4 *Mrs. Lewis late Miss Hervey as William Tell* [*c.* 1833?]. This was a benefit-night stunt. Penny portrait no. 2 shows the same actress as Richard the Third

87. Halfpenny portrait no. 103 *Mr. J. B. Howe as William Tell* [1862–72]. The other portrait of Mrs Lewis was converted to halfpenny portrait no. 101 *Mr. C. Dillon as Richard the Third*

88. Halfpenny combats nos 11/12 [later 1830s] and halfpenny portraits nos 71/72 [end of 1830s], Hiam's address being given as Johns Row and Ratcliffe Row respectively

89. Halfpenny portraits nos 5/6 *Mr. Ducrow as the Brigand* and *as Jack Junk*, halfpenny fours nos 15/16 and (pantomime) fours nos 1[7?]/18 [all mid-1830s]. In the same collection

another double plate of Skelt's fours has strange ghostly impressions of various Hiam marks

90. *Paul Clifford* ch. 1–8, sc. 2–4, 7

91. Portrait no. 46 *Madame Auriol as Columbine*

92. *Fours* of Mr. J. Alexander as Harlequin, *etc.*

93. David Drakard and Paul Holdway, *Spode Transfer Printed Ware 1784–1833: A new, enlarged and updated edition* (2002), pp. 56–59, including photographs of marks and an excellent illustration of a copper and brass works in Shoe Lane (the Whittow works taken over and enlarged by Pontifex??). See also p. 55 for an illustration of copper plates stacked upright (but naked) in wooden pigeon-holes against a brick wall

94. *The Forest of Bondy* sc. 1 (26 Dec 1846)

95. *The Sleeping Beauty* ch. 5 (26 Dec 1850)

96. *Blackbeard the Pirate* wg 34 (18 Nov 1851) [recto, at side and bottom], *Whittington and his Cat* sc. 7 (26 Dec 1853) [verso, at side] and *Rob Roy* sc. 2 (26 Dec 1855) [recto]

97. *Black Eyed Susan* ch. 1–7, sc. 6 (14 Dec 1840), *Aladdin* ch. 1–8 (1 Jan 1841), *The Maid and the Magpie* ch. 1–5, sc. 1, 5 (1 Jul 1841)

98. *Aladdin* sc. 1, 2, 5, 6, 8, 12 (1 Jan 1841)

99. A great deal has been written about the family, including Robert R. Toomey, *Vivian and Sons, 1809–1924: A Study of the Firm in the Copper and Related Industries* (1985)

100. *Encyclopaedia Britannica*, 11th edition (1910–11) *s.v.* Zinc

101. Portrait no. 14 (new series) *Mr. Dry as Lambro the Pirate* [1837], sixes no. 22 [1837], 24 (26 Dec 1837)

102. Portrait no. 11 (new series) *Mr. Butler as Caractacas the British Chieftain* (4 Dec 1837) [mark on two corners], sixes no. 17 (6 Mar 1837), no. 18 (27 Mar 1837) [mark in centre and on all four corners], small sixes no. IV [undated, but same period as the others]

103. Portrait no. 2 (new series) *Mr. Lee as the Green Knight* [1837], where perhaps PROVAL is the beginning of PRO VALORE, the crown being one awarded "for valour"

104. Portrait no. 68 *Miss E. Tree as Ion* [1836]

105. *Top Borders* (1 Apr 1833)

106. *Jonathan Bradford* sc. 7 (29 Aug 1833)

107. *Jonathan Bradford* wg 2 (29 Aug 1833)

108. Portrait no. 11 *Mr. Grimaldi as Clown. Illuminating the Entrance to Old Gutter Lane* (16 Feb 1833)

109. [Drop scene, date and full title unknown, but afterwards converted to *The Brigand* sc. 7, and re-dated 19 Sep 1836]. As Dodie Masterman pointed out many years ago, the drop scene was itself copied from a previously-published view: see George Speaight, "The Brigand in the Toy Theatre", in *The Saturday Book* 29 (1969), pp. 204–215

110. *Orchestra* (3 Aug 1834) and wg 1 (21 Aug 1834), giving us the top left and top right portions respectively

111. *Douglas* sc. 1, 4, 5, wg 2 (1 Nov 1834), where sc. 4 and 5 give the top left and top centre of one print, and wg 2 the top centre of another

112. *Combat in Chevy Chase* [date removed by Webb, but apparently in the same style as combats nos 2 and 3 in *Jack Sheppard* and in *Jane of the Hatchet*, both dated 1 Mar 1849].

Combat no. 3 is on a plate narrower than usual, and the names of the combating figures have had to be omitted in consequence. Green was evidently running out of sheet zinc, cutting corners, and looking round his premises for re-usable old coppers

113. *Wapping Old Stairs* sc. 7 (1 Feb 1838)

114. *The Battle of Waterloo* ch. 8 (18 June 1842)

115. *The Battle of Waterloo* ch. 9 (18 June 1842)

116. [Small valentine of lady with bird, undated]

117. *Whittington and his Cat* sc. 9, 10, 12 (26 Dec 1853)

118. *The Daughter of the Regiment* ch. 1, 2, 3, sc. 1 (1 Sep 1857), giving clubs, spades, diamonds, hearts, respectively (all copper, though sc. 2, the only new plate used in the play, is zinc, as would be expected at this period)

119. *Goody Goose* ch. 1, 3–9, sc. 1–13 [*c*. 1859]

120. *Goody Goose* ch. 2 [*c*. 1859]

121. *The Mistletoe Bough* ch. 2, 3 (old version), used respectively for *Fours* of Count Rudolph etc. and for *New Sixteens* No. 5; and *The Waterman* ch. 1, 2, used respectively for *Mr. G. Clair as Matthioli* and for *The Waterman* ch. 1 (new version)

122. *Blue Beard* ch. 2

123. *Blue Beard* ch. 5

124. *Blue Beard* ch. 6

125. *Blue Beard* sc. 1

126. [Plate of fairies]

127. Used respectively for *Mr. Anderson as Macbeth* (which at least preserves the Scotch association) and *Mr. Creswick as Hamlet* (which doesn't). The latter re-usage seems to have upset Redington's numbering system, the portrait being given the number 112, which is also the number of *Mr. C. Pitt as Caleb Crook*, part of the sequence 110–113, four portraits from the Britannia Theatre drama *Robert la Grange*

128. Sixes no. 14 and *Skelt's Horse and Foot Band* no. 3 respectively

129. Frontispiece to *Richard Turpin* [*c*. 1835]

130. Frontispiece to *Mary the Maid of the Inn* [*c*. 1835]

131. Frontispiece to *Der Freischutz* [*c*. 1840]

132. Frontispiece to *Aladdin* [early 1840s]

133. *Mr. T. P. Cooke as Marmaduke Morgan* [sic, though the character is usually called Dorgan] and *Mr. T. P. Cooke as Harry Hallyard* (Carr 1840s?, then Bishop 1850s?)

134. See the print of the orginal Carr version of *Mr. T. P. Cooke. as Arthur Bright* in the Barry Clarke collection, also the plate of *Mr. C. Freer. as Wolfender* in the Morice Collection, where "arr" can be glimpsed under "Bishop & Co."; and note that in all the Bishop ex Carr plates the erasure (and knocking-up) only ever covers half of the new name

135. See Eddie Cass, *The Lancashire Pace-Egg Play: A Social History* (2001), pp. 140–141

136. *The Silver Palace* ch. 5 (5 Sep 1841)

137. *The Wreck Ashore* sc. 2, 3, 6, 8, wg 18, 19 (1 Jun 1837) and the plate converted by Green to create *The Lord Mayor's Fool* sc. 3 (1 Apr 1837)

138. *Whittington and his Cat* sc. 9 (26 Dec 1853)

139. *Harlequin Oliver Cromwell* sc. 11 (26 Dec 1852)

140. *Baron Munchausen* sc. 8 (*c*. 1859)

141. *Dred* (26 Dec 1856)

142. *Blue Beard* (1 Dec 1837) sc. 4, 5, 8, 10, 11, 12

143. *King Henry; or, The Miller of Mansfield* (early 1860s) ch. 3

144. *Harlequin and Guy Fawkes* (26 Dec 1836) ch. 1

145. Webb's *Opera Polka* and *Original Polka*, and his *Comicalties* nos 1–6

146. Part of a stage front, and three double plates: *My Poll and my Partner Joe* sc. 12 and wg; *The Rover's Bride* sc. 11 (set pieces) and wg; *The Waterman* sc. 1/3

147. Reproduced in Speaight, p. 118, no. 8, and in West catalogue, p. 7, fig. 1

148. I suggest that *Miss Vincent as Agnes Primrose* [1841/42?], signed "Gunthorpe sc", was given away with no. 2 (new series) of *The Star*. Copy (formerly owned by George Speaight) in the Robinson collection, though the details given in Speaight, p. 200 (with Star as a penny-packet publisher of the 1880s, operating from Gunthorpe Square), seem to be based on a series of misinterpretations

149. J. B. Howe, *A Cosmpolitan Actor* (1888), quoted in Speaight, p. 134

150. Its portrait no. 1 *Mr. Fraser as Dick Turpin* is difficult to date, but no. 3 *Mr. T. P. Cooke as Union Jack* is the same subject as Park's first lithographic portrait, and no. 2 *Mr. Saville as Jack Sheppard* is also suggestive of the early 1840s

151. W. S. Fortey's New Halfpenny Characters, the ones seen (formerly owned by George Speaight, and now in the Robinson collection) being equestrian portraits of *General Garibaldi* and *King of Naples*, *Lord Clyde* (suppressor of the Indian mutiny, ennobled 1858) and *Lord Elcho* (promoter of the Rifle Volunteers, 1859)

152. Halfpenny portraits nos 183/184 [1843?], 261/262 [late 1840s], 273/274 [c.1850], of which 183/184 *Mr. T. P. Cooke as Union Jack* and *Mr. Hicks as Mordenbrenner* are the same two subjects as nos 1 and 2 of the penny lithographic series

153. Two of these prints are in that part of the Speaight collection now owned by Peter Baldwin, and the plate for another in the Morice Collection: see p. 17

154. The different practices of Redington and Pollock are explained in a very informative article by Samuel Pollock (son of Benjamin) in *Pollock's World of Toys* [c. 1970], p. 3

155. "The Juvenile Builder" bears a device dated 1862, but Myers could have used this over a long period, so the toys may not themselves be so early

156. *Blue Beard* ch. 3, 7, 9; some twenty-five portraits; and also *Pollock's New Policemen*

157. *Baron Munchausen* sc. 10 = *The Mistletoe Bough* sc. 7 [the words "Scene" and "No." only], *The Mistletoe Bough* sc. 5, 6

158. *Twelves* no. 85 of Napier, etc., *Twelves* (unnumbered) of Champion, etc.

159. *Baron Munchausen* sc. 3, 5, [below-deck nautical scene of uncertain purpose], [sheet of fairies], portrait no. 181 *Sir Brian*; large scenes in *The Silver Palace* sc. 1–4, top drops, wg 24; large scenes in *The Daughter of the Regiment* sc. 1–2; large exotic tree wings; and large orchestra

160. *Fours* of Mr. Pitt as Prophet King, *etc.*

161. *Jack the Giant Killer* ch. 3

162. *Oliver Twist* sc. 6 (ROB ROY at right hand), sc. 11 (WHITTINGTON AND HIS CAT at left hand and RIDDLE ME RIDDLE ME REE at right hand), sc. 13 (JACK THE GIANT KILLER at left hand and OLIVER CROMWELL at right hand), wg 3 (THE DAUGHTER OF THE REGIMENT and TRICKS both at right hand) [left and right hand as printed, not as engraved]

163. *Blue Beard* ch. 6, right hand [as printed]

164. same as previous note

165. The day after the performance of *The Miller and his Men* given (in memoriam Georgii et Mariae Speaight) at the Theatre Museum

166. *Blackbeard the Pirate* ch. 4

167. *The Panthen* [sic], reproduced in Thomas Gretton, *Murders and Moralities: English Catchpenny Prints, 1800–1860* (1980), no. 56, pp. 90–91

168. Wilson, opp, p. 58

169. Mayhew interview 1850/1972, p. 117

170. Other interesting registrations include John Bailey 1799, 1807, 1825, Mrs Sarah Bailey 1806, and Joseph Bailey 1824; John Pitts 1808; John Fairburn 1819, and George Fairburn 1837; William Hodgson 1820, 1822, and Bernard Hodgson 1820, 1821, 1825; Thomas Goode senior 1829, and Thomas Goode junior 1829, 1839 (more than one press), 1841 (ditto), 1846 (ditto), 1859 (ditto); John Vandenberg Quick 1832 (ditto); Eleazar Lazarus 1834; Frederick Edwards 1835; John Shorman 1846; and.William Spencer Johnson 1861 (steam power presses). See William B. Todd, *A Directory of Printers and Others in Allied Trades, London and Vicinity, 1800–1840* (1972), *s.vv.*

171. Julius Berstl, *The Sun's Bright Child: The Imaginary Memoirs of Edmund Kean* [1946], opp. p. 128

172. For the effects of this on surviving copies of the Webb plays, see my Historical Note to the "Holt" reprint of Skelt's *Pizarro*

173. The identity of the colourist had long been suspected by Barry Clarke, but I am indebted to Hugo Brown for finding proof of this

174. For Lucy Adlam, see Jan Piggott's "Two Pence Coloured", below, p. 70

TWO PENCE COLOURED

J. R. Piggott

In boyhood I spoiled many sheets of penny plain toy theatre engravings, both characters and scenes, with my coloured inks. Winter evenings were spent with over-subtle colours and a jeweller's care over tiny details such as belts or buttons. The juvenile artist was in effect a vandal amateur; nor did the detail register when the characters were mounted, cut out with nail scissors and put into a tin slide behind the proscenium. The boy applied himself to genteel refinements at the table with bottles, saucers and brushes, but the professional 'twopence coloured' sheets, with their bold colours and bold tracts occluding the fine points of the engraving, sent much better images to the eye at the proper distance from the stage. Years later I read an essay by the Victorian social historian John Ashton called 'Childhood's Drama' in his book *Varia*, published in 1894:

> The characters, scenes, wings, &c., were sold in sheets to suit the different sizes of the theatres, from one halfpenny each to threepence or fourpence plain, but double that price if they were coloured. No amateur could compete with the professional colourist; his best and most artistic efforts were tame and vapid in comparison, for he lacked the vivid colours of the professional, and especially was he wanting in boldness. Were it a garden scene, the colourist selected his brightest crimson lake for the roses, or he might paint them Prussian blue, which was quite as effective; whilst the brilliancy of the green was unattainable by any combination of gamboge and Prussian blue. Nor could the amateur aspire to vie with his rival in costume. There, again, his reds were redder, his blues bluer, and although he never used many colours, yet those he did employ were the most effective and satisfying to the eye. True, the amateur might paint some of his roses pink, and shade them with red, leave some white, and paint some of delicate Maréchal Niel tint, and also he would not paint beyond the limits of the flower; but

Above: illustration by John Leech for Albert Smith's novel *Christopher Tadpole* (1848), showing a toy theatre displayed for sale in a small newsagent's (JP)

Left and right: part of John Leech's series of illustrations, *Young Troublesome* (1845), showing toy theatre sheets being coloured at home (JP)

65

Top: portrait [1831] by T. J. Brown, for whom see Horatio Blood's "Tinsel", below, p. 73 (AP). *Above*: characters (after Robert Cruikshank's drawings) from Orlando Hodgson's *The Siege of Troy; or, The Giant Horse* (1833) (AP). *Below*: characters in Webb's *Aladdin* [early 1880s], re-issued by lithography from the plates of Skelt [early 1840s] (AP)

the gaudy blotches of the professional were the most telling, and took a tithe part of the time to do. As in the major theatre of grown-up life, if you, dear reader, were to try your maiden hand at scene-painting, you would make a melancholy failure, the coarse daubs of those who have made it their study, telling in front with far greater effect. [pp. 4–5]

Robert Louis Stevenson's famous essay 'A Penny Plain and Twopence Coloured' (1884) with its call to 'speed to Pollock's . . . if you love art, folly, or the bright eyes of children', I knew by heart. At Pollock's shop in Monmouth Street I bought a copy of the essay which they had reprinted as a pamphlet in a dark blue paper cover with a die-cut oval revealing a vignette of a harlequin figure printed in sanguine. Stevenson makes a feeble admission that the honey was sucked after he had coloured the prints; I was proud that I habitually followed the process of preparation from colouring through to performance:

I cannot deny that joy attended the illumination; nor can I quite forgive that child who, wilfully foregoing pleasure, stoops to 'twopence coloured'. With crimson lake (hark to the sound of it – crimson lake! – the horns of elfland are not richer on the ear) – with crimson lake and Prussian blue a certain purple is to be compounded which, for cloaks especially, Titian could not equal. The latter colour with gamboge, a hated name although an exquisite pigment, supplied a green of such a savoury greenness that today my heart regrets it. Nor can I recall without a tender weakness the very aspect of the water where I dipped my brush. Yes, there was pleasure in the painting. But when all was painted, it is needless to deny it, all was spoiled. You might, indeed, set up a scene or two simply to look at; but to cut the figures out was simply sacrilege; nor could any child twice court the tedium, the worry, and the long-drawn disenchantment of an actual performance. Two days after the purchase the honey had been sucked. [*Memories and Portraits*, (1887), 1906, p. 219–20.]

In a novel of 1848, *The Struggles and Adventures of Christopher Tadpole at Home and Abroad*, by Albert Smith (1816–60), a follower of Dickens, the disenchantment of juvenile efforts to colour theatrical portraits at home is moralised as a preparation for life's disappointments:

> There were colour boxes in Sprouts's shop window; but they only contained the paints of childhood – little hard gritty squares of some composition, which usually refused to be rubbed on the back of a plate at all with any effect; but if they did, all gave one colour whatever their hue, and that was generally a dull bricky red. But for a penny what could be expected! The sixpenny sets to be sure were in varnished sliding boxes, with a pocket-book view on the top, to colour which, the first endeavours of the young artists usually tended, before they aspired to Mr. Hicks as the Wizard of the Wave; but these also were of the same disappointing manufacture; and even when finished with the greatest care and nicest eye to effect, Mr Hicks had a washed-out appearance, which suggested that the wave of which he was the wizard, had great power over him. The children sighed for the brilliant hues of the 'twopence coloured' prints – for the dazzling red of the couch on which the young lady with the short waist and ringlets was asleep, on the frontispiece of the dream-books – for the bright blue that made the frock-coated lover on the valentine so captivating – for the ruby crimson of the port wine on the Twelfth Night characters, that swelled beyond the outline of the decanter. But these were never attainable. Perhaps it was as well; for it mingled instruction with amusement, and read a lesson to the young artists in their earliest years, how futile it was to think that anything would wear the same bright tints in reality, as those with which the prismatic anticipations of youth invested it. [p. 386]

Roy Strong, a toy theatre enthusiast in his youth, wrote in *The Times* for 14 January 1967 about the almost psychedelic effect of professional colouring on the scenes:

> Twopence brought with it luscious, at times almost aggressive colour. An unfaded dream world of primary colours in which all clouds are pink, skies strident blue, flowers crimson and yellow, and life is lived out against an eternal sunset.

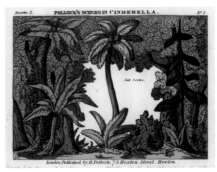

There are two sources of information about the techniques used by the colourists employed by the toy theatre publishers: an oral tradition passed down from the last of them, and the studies written in the 1930s and 1940s. George Speaight had examined many examples of coloured toy theatre sheets from all periods, and wrote in 1946 in *Juvenile Drama*:

From top to bottom: unlettered proof from West's *The Ruffian Boy* (1819), with directions to the colourist. Three hand-coloured sheets as analysed by Stan Bult in 1941 (BC): Pollock's *Cinderella* sc. 2 (originally Green 1849), *Baron Munchausen* sc. 13 (Redington [1859]), *Pollock's New Pantomime Characters* no. 4 (mainly selected from Green)

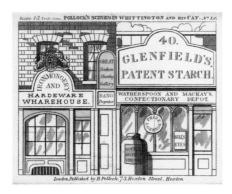

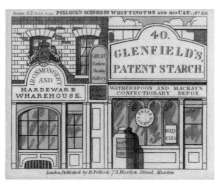

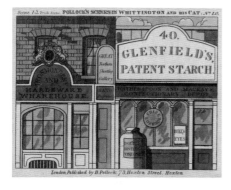

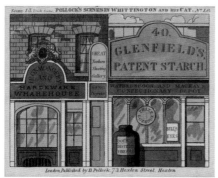

Scene in Pollock's *Whittington and his Cat* (originally Green 1853), coloured by Kate Irvine to show the stages of the hand-colouring process (BC)

The quality of colouring follows the quality of printing; with West, Jameson, and Hodgson, it is exquisite, with Orlando Hodgson less exquisite, but more dramatic; with Skelt less careful, but still thrilling. Green's colours stood no chance on his cheap paper, but the old flamboyance was there, and those of his plays coloured only a few years ago in the authentic manner by Miss Pollock, still shine as 'gorgeous as summer flowers'. It is only in the coloured sheets that the Juvenile Drama attains its full charm; how was this brilliant colouring achieved?

In the first place the materials were of the best. West claims that his plays were 'printed on fine drawing paper purposely for colouring', and simply to feel this old paper is a pleasure in itself. In later years the 'wrong' side of the paper was sometimes printed, as it held the colours better. And then the colours, like the printing inks, were not bought at shops, but specially mixed to old and secret formulas, and applied while still fresh. A great mystery was made of the colouring, and many were the rumours of the secret ingredients that were added to obtain such bright hues; gum, sugar, and a few drops of beer, it was said, were mixed to make the yellow gleam as if it was burnished, and the crimson make blood, in comparison, look like water. I cannot refrain from boasting that I have been honoured to receive from Miss Pollock and from Mr How Matthews, two of the last surviving publishers of the Juvenile Drama, their own special recipes for mixing their colours. But in these days, when every printseller in town has his private establishment for turning one pound plain into two pounds coloured, wild horses would not drag the secret from me! [1946, p. 86]

The toy theatre sheets were coloured by children or families guided by a coloured proof; as in the decadence of manuscript illumination in the workshops at Bruges in the late Middle Ages this craft was a collaboration, to each colourist his own colour, down a long table or around a circular one. Andrew Tuer wrote in 1898 in his *Pages and Pictures from Forgotten Children's Books*:

The colouring was done by children in their teens, who worked with astonishing celerity and more precision than could be expected. They sat round a table, each with a little pan of water-colour, a brush, a partly coloured copy as a guide, and a pile of printed sheets. One child would paint on the red, wherever it appeared in the copy; another followed, say, with the yellow, and so on until the colouring was finished. [p. 6]

Recent research by David Powell has taught us that since William West (1783–1854), on the basis of a remark in an interview given to Henry Mayhew, appears to have disapproved of child labour, he most likely used skilled and relatively well-paid adults for his colouring, called by Powell 'dashing and vigorous, yet at times exquisite'; W. G. Webb (1821–1890) relied on families, from four families to at one point as many as twelve. [David Powell, et al, '*William West and the Regency Toy Theatre*, 2004, p. 21; David Powell, *W. G. Webb and the Victorian Toy Theatre*, 2005, p. 34]

Mr. How Matthews told George Speaight of the methods of the colourists employed by his family at the end of the nineteenth century:

> Speed would come with practice; a pair of legs would be done with one stroke of the brush, starting up one leg and down the other, narrowing and widening the brush, in about two seconds; about the same time for a jacket, right and left arm. The whole figure would take about eight seconds. A sheet of characters, say eighty seconds, or say, a gross of 144 sheets would take four to six hours; at two shillings a gross this would work out at fourpence an hour. [Speaight, 1946, pp. 87–8]

The actual colours used varied of course over the years and according to the house style of the publishers, but the authorities concur that they were mixed from only three or four. A. E. Wilson, writing in 1932, said that four colours were used: gamboge, Prussian blue, carmine and black, and that sugar was added for a rich oily sheen. [*Penny Plain, Twopence Coloured*, p. 42] George Speaight made a record of several uncoloured proof sheets in the British Museum with William West's directions to the colourist; for one sheet of characters West indicated red, copper, dark brown, yellow, black, flesh, buff, light blue, steel, brown, pink, and white. One was marked 'colours a great deal brighter.' [p. 87]

Stanley Bult's article, 'Colouring the Juvenile Drama', (*British Puppet and Model Theatre Guild, 11th Wartime Bulletin*, Worcester, October 1941) tells us the most about colouring in the later historical period; he also discusses

Left: Redington portrait [*c.* 1860], colouring guide kept with the set of stencils (BC). *Right*: stencil [1880s??] used to colour the blue parts of the portrait, with reverse, showing reinforcement of torn or weak parts (BC)

how stencils were used for speed in the heyday of cheap sheets and by Benjamin Pollock, some of whose stencils have survived:

> If you have examined the coloured sheets of the Juvenile Drama, you must have been struck by their wide variety of tints and tones. True, one scene has only 4, but most show from 10 to 15 distinct colours. In one scene from *Cinderella* I counted 4 browns, 4 blues, 2 yellows, 2 pinks, 2 greens, one each red, violet and grey, in all 17 distinct colours. All these were produced from three basic watercolours! Scene 13 in *Baron Munchausen* has 167 separate pieces of colouring; in 'Pantomime Characters', Sheet 4, there are 122. To make the colouring a commercial proposition stencilling was resorted to. Stencil-plate cutting is an art in itself. Usually the two methods (stencilling and application of colour by sable 'pencils' [brushes]) are used in combination. In any case, they must be bold because the area of colour is so small.
>
> The three basic colours are Carmine, Gamboge and Light Chinese Blue. They are obtained in dry form, gamboge in a lump, the others as powders. The blue needs a small addition of gum to the water, but the gamboge is merely rubbed up in plain water. The preparation of carmine however is more complicated. The powder is shaken up in a mixture of water and ammonia. The glass jar is exposed to daylight for a fortnight with frequent shaking, when the dye will be extracted.
>
> The lighter tints are put in first, practice alone leading to an even 'wash'. Added touches give variations. The typical brilliant crimson is produced by applying deep pink over strong yellow. [pp. 9–10]

Stencils might number as many as seven cut boards for seven colours. There was a danger of the stencil slipping with impatient use.

The last professional colourist was the legendary Lucy Adlam, who is to be seen in the illustration by Peter Jackson in *The Evening News* for 13 Dec 1950; she passed on her skills to Dodie Masterman, who passed them on to Kate Irvine.

Lucy Adlam, drawn by Peter Jackson for his *Evening News* strip, "London is Stranger than Fiction" (1950) (JP)

TINSEL

Horatio Blood

"You see the cheap shops makes up the dresses with silk, and tinsel, and foil, but I never did. My customers used to do some; but to my mind, it spoilt the figures, and took away all the good drawing from 'em. Formerly they used to cut out the parts of the figures, and stick pieces of silk, and tinsel, and lace behind them. Then the boys used to make all their own dots and ornaments themselves; and I used to sell punches expressly for doing 'em, and arter that I sold the ornaments themselves. Now the ornaments are sold in large quantities by these printsellers. They are punched out by children I think – they make them as low as a halfpenny a packet."[1]

Thus William West, 'the aristocrat among theatrical stationers',[2] displayed his disdain for tinsel pictures to Henry Mayhew in 1850, though ironically the earliest surviving example of contemporary tinselling appears on one of his portraits. Apparently dating from 1823, it depicts Edmund Kean as Richard III and incorporates velvet and silk from the Coronation robes of George IV.[3]

The practice of embellishing engraved portraits with pieces of cloth and lace dates back to the 'patch portraits' of the eighteenth century,[4] while even some of the earliest prints were sprinkled with spangled stuff, as surviving late fourteenth-century German popular woodcuts attest.[5] Tinsel pictures seized on these ideas by making a marriage of fabric and foil and enriching both with an unrestrained theatrical panache. West's account reveals that the idea was initiated by the public who purchased metal foil from the jeweller (used as backing for paste jewellery) and cut it to shape to fit the portrait themselves.[6] The next stage came with the stamped dots for which the punches were sold by West. Excellent results were achieved with combinations of cut foil and artistically arranged dots, the latter providing a dimension of depth. The final flourish was the invention of the professionally made theatrical ornaments that typify the true tinsel picture. These die-stamped embossed decorations, punched from paper-backed copper foil, were available in a brilliant array of colours and an infinite variety of designs, the neo-classical nature of many of them closely resembling the cast iron foundryman's catalogue in miniature.[7]

The earliest theatrical portraits do not, with a handful of exceptions, lend themselves to be tinselled; however, during the late 1820s the dazzling demands of the public began to affect the art of the print publishers. It is difficult to ascribe this trend to any particular publisher, but it is certainly apparent in the portraits of Bailey whose attitudes became more exaggerated and costumes more richly detailed. The desire for ornamentation was also echoed in the lettering, with florid Tuscan forms finding favour over the Roman ones used by West. But this was merely the

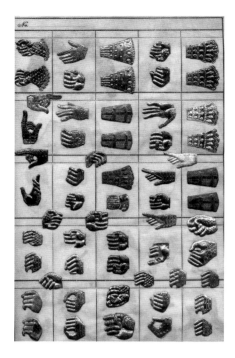 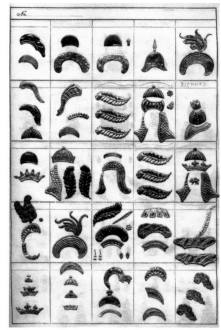 

Above and across: pages from a tinsel sample book, bought by Desmond Seaton-Reid from "Young Harry" Webb, showing the cornucopia of shapes and colours kept in stock (KI)

overture to the Williamite glories of the 1830s, when the extravagantly engraved excesses of Robert Cruikshank's portraits for Orlando Hodgson and John Fairburn, designed specifically for theatrical ornaments, elevated tinselling to the heights of the gods.[8] The *theatrical* gave way to the *dramatic* as Regency elegance was upstaged by shimmering spectacle and a new native popular art emerged.

One of the earliest announcements for tinselling requisites dates from 1829 and appears on the cover of the book of words for *Black-Eyed Susan* published by Richard Lloyd at his Juvenile Dramatic Repository, 40 Gibson Street, near the Coburg Theatre, who lists 'Theatrical Ornaments, Foil and Gold Papers'.[9] The following year Lloyd expanded the theme in his delightful doggerel advertisement 'The Invitation' with its fourth verse devoted to tinselling portraits:

> You who, admiring these Ladies and Gentlemen,
> Wish to see each of them splendidly drest,
> May, for a trifle ('tis scarcely worth mentioning)
> Have them in velvet and silk of the best;
> Ornaments of each kind, such as will suit your mind,
> Here you may cheaply find, of every hue;
> Crowns, Stars, and Suns so bright, yellow, green, red
>   or white –
> And, what's more, ev'ry week he brings out something
>   new.[10]

This demonstrates that, even at this early date, Lloyd supplied not only the ornaments but also the pre-shaped pieces of fabric with which to dress or 'silk' the portrait.[11] Two rather elusive figures were describing them-

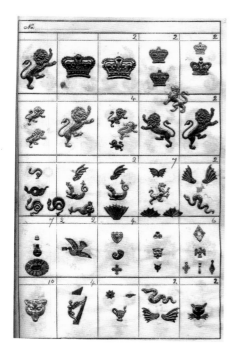 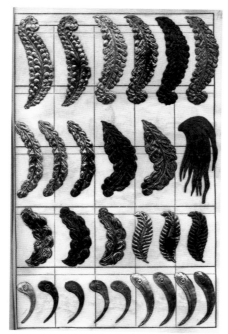

selves as 'Theatrical Ornament Makers' in the early 1830s: Eleazer Lazarus and T. J. Brown, at least one of whose prints includes the tantalising boast: 'All the Ornaments for this Portrait may be had of T. J. BROWN, the Original Inventor. A Variety of New & Elegant Patterns are now in preparation.'[12]

Continuing research may yet cast new light on these shadowy origins but for all the early developments, the undisputed King of Tinsel was James Webb, the gunsmith uncle of W. G. Webb, who according to long-cherished juvenile drama lore was 'the first man to make the steel punches for stamping out the tinsel ornaments'.[13] Webb did not style himself 'Theatrical Ornament Maker' until the late 1830s, almost a decade after Lloyd's advertisement, so the chronology at first appears dubious. Webb, however, is traditionally credited with the manufacture of the dies and not the invention of tinselling *in toto*. It is perfectly feasible he could have made and supplied dies to Brown and others as he was established as a gunsmith by 1831 and may have been working as such at a slightly earlier date.[14] What is undoubtedly true is that James Webb organised and exploited tinselling to such an extent that his family dominated the trade for a century, although tinselled examples of portraits actually published by Webb are few and far between. The importance of the house of Webb is demonstrated by the great tinsel pattern book, the existence of which was first revealed by W. G. Webb in 1889:

"But stay, I will show you something I have never shown to a stranger before. I have a book here which I know to be absolutely unique. There is not another like it in existence, and there never was. But it will give you an idea of the extent of the business in its palmy days."

Mr Webb thereupon fetched from a back room what looked like a

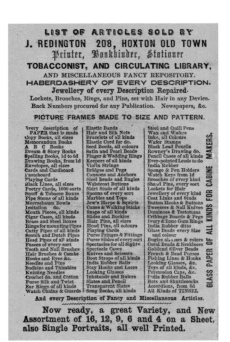

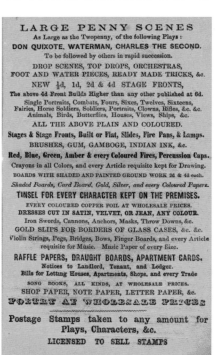

Top right: advertising station [*c.* 1859], showing Redington's advertisement for his shaded boards (DP). *Top left and above*: advertisement from the inside wrapper of a Redington book of words [early 1860s], showing silk, tinsel, shaded boards, and all the other impedimenta of tinselling for sale (AP)

big ledger carefully wrapped in a cloth bag. It was a ledger, and it had a spring clasp upon it, to keep out prying eyes. Opening this big book before the astonished eyes of our representative there appeared rows upon rows of tiny tinselled swords, shields, hilts, helmets, glaives, gauntlets, buttons, belts, daggers, pistols, boots, feathers, and every possible kind of ornament all arranged in marvellously neat array from one end to the other of the great book.

"There," said the old gentleman, after the book had been admired and apostrophised, "that was my pattern book. It was made by my wife while I was courting her. [They married in 1845.] There will never be such another, for the dies are mostly destroyed, and will never be made again."[15]

Between its red calf boards this book contains an Aladdin's cave of '1,919 different specimens of tinsel ornaments, each offered in a variety of colours, so that there are, in all, over 13,000 different ornaments mounted in the volume',[16] 'the steel dies for which cost nearly four thousand pounds'.[17] This seems an astonishing amount of money but as 3,250 different dies survive in the Webb archive (and more are said to have been lost) perhaps it is not so far off the mark.[18] It must also be remembered that tinselling was an expensive business:

Take, for instance, Mr. Kean as Richard III. A young tinseller would have to buy a special crown at a cost, say, of ninepence or a shilling; a special sword, say fourpence; special gloves and boots, and belt and many dots (at twopence or fourpence a packet); so that a tinselled picture had an intrinsic as well as an art value.

Jonathan King, the stationer and compulsive collector, recorded 'that the ornaments to finish a picture cost 8s. or 10s.'.[20] In its heyday tinselling must have been a highly profitable line for the juvenile drama publishers by which they were able to transform a halfpenny, penny or twopenny print into several shillings worth of tinsel. This probably played a large part in propping up the toy theatre side of the business.

James Webb is named as agent on the portraits published in the 1850s and 1860s by John Redington of Hoxton who sold 'All kinds of TINSEL. Boards for shaded and painted groundwork 2d or 4d each. Shaded Boards, Card Board, Gold, Silver, and every Coloured Papers. Dresses cut in satin, velvet or jean, any colour. Every coloured copper foil at whole-sale prices. Tinsel for every character kept on the premises.'[21] Despite this, and the fact that his daughter Eliza (the future Mrs Benjamin Pollock) was a dab hand at applying the theatrical ornaments,[22] tinselled examples of Redington's portraits are unusual, though he seems to have cornered the market with his particular painted backgrounds, bearing his imprint, on which the finished portraits were mounted. Their heavy black outlines and jolly naivety have an affinity with the popular picturesque of cottage glass paintings and narrow boat castles, but seem closer in spirit to the traditional backcloths for Sicilian puppet theatres, and indeed the wild-eyed marionettes from Palermo encased in richly embossed shimmering metal armour are surely the animated incarnations of tinsel pictures.[23]

The last theatrical portraits were published in the 1860s and the 'palmy days' were now decidedly autumnal, though winter was, amazingly, still

Left: shaded board for *Mr G. Almar as the Water King* as sold by Redington [*c.* 1860] (BC). *Right*: Park's penny fours no. 6 (1839), for one of which Redington's little "shaded board" was intended (BC)

Shaded boards for *Speckbacker* and for *Mr Osbaldiston as Grindoff* as sold by Redington [*c.* 1860] (BC)

eighty years off. As the toy theatre declined, so did tinselling, though the ornaments were put to other seasonal uses such as decorating Valentines or effigies of Guy Fawkes for Bonfire Night. The old publishers were hit hard by the steam-driven competition of the Penny Dreadfuls which were not only treading the boards themselves with wood-engraved characters and scenes but by the 1870s were promising, with shameless – though admirable – hyperbole '£5 worth of Tinsel given to every subscriber'.[24] Despite this, James Webb continued to make theatrical ornaments until his death in 1881, after which his mantle was assumed by his great-nephew H. J. Webb, and in the late 1880s A. How Mathews of Acton was advertising 'superior tinsel in various colours' at '1d a sheet' on his books of words. In 1894 John Ashton referred to tinselling as 'an art now dead',[25] but it wouldn't lie down, and in 1926 Webb made some new tinsel pictures for the exhibition of his toy theatre collection at the Faculty of Arts Gallery which led to a new demand and a revival of the trade. The Webbs drew on their extensive stocks of portraits (principally the Johnson ex-Fairburn ones) and the dies and miniature mangles used to emboss the fish-scale armour were once again wheeled into service. In 1932, Mr Webb was even filmed at work by Pathé for their newsreel *Tinsel Pictures*.[26] These late flowerings are among the finest tinsel pictures ever made: the portraits dripping with tinsel against skyscapes of a celestial superiority. But this revival seems to have been overlooked by A. E. Wilson who wrote that 'For many years it has been impossible to obtain these ornaments.'[27]

Stocks of tinsel were exhausted even earlier at Hoxton Street, as Grace Lovat Fraser recalled:

> Even as recently as 1920 I can remember buying some bits of these special foil trimmings in old Mr Pollock's shop in Hoxton with which to trim some of the prints which he still made from the original plates; but his stock was then very low and quite irreplaceable.[28]

The sale of tinsel, however, was not solely confined to London, and Emma Lomax[29] remembered

> a little shop in Brighton. It was smaller than Pollock's, and, I think, very dirty; but it was the very gate of Heaven to one little girl . . . The things one could buy in that shop! Frost, tinsel, dots and stars, some stuff called Lawn Green in little pill-boxes.[30]

Years later Miss Lomax went to Bumpus's where the effect of seeing George Speaight's performance of *The Miller and his Men* in 1933 sent her 'hotfoot to Hoxton. Pollock's was so like the little Brighton shop, except for the absence of tinsel, dots and stars (gone, alas, for ever).'[31]

H. J. Webb died the same year and although his son Young Harry was 'a very fine tinseller who could colour in the traditional style' it seems that no more tinsel pictures were made after the mid-thirties thus ending a century of family tradition.[32] It is probable that the tinsel revival was brought to an abrupt end not through a lack of demand, but simply because the stocks of foil paper had run out and could not be replenished.[33] And here we arrive at the great tinselling mystery, the Coade stone enigma of the juvenile drama: the unknown process by which the copper foil was backed with paper. This was essential to glue the ornament to the portrait and the secret is said to have died with either W. G. Webb or his uncle James.[34] Many of the surviving sheets of unused tinsel foil are not paper-backed, though this practical deficiency gives them a highly pleasing tinnily-toned rattle when gently shaken. But from whence did the Webbs obtain the foil? It seems likely that it was supplied by Isaac Bousquet of the Barbican who was by 1883 the sole manufacturer in London of 'gold, silver and foil papers and tin foil in all colours' and who certainly handled 'metal-faced papers' so perhaps the secret in fact died with him.[35] Webb's tools for the tinselling trade were quietly forgotten until they re-emerged at Sotheby's in 1994.[36] Despite this, valiant efforts have been made over the years to recreate the art (mostly using substitute foil imported from the Continent) by enthusiasts such as John Noble, Ian Sargint, Debby Brown and Joseph Hope Williams.

True tinsel pictures have never been 'unconsidered trifles', having always had their devotees. Indeed, as the book illustrator Harry Furniss was already collecting them in the 1890s they were at the forefront of the Victorian Revival, and the toy theatre itself is the constant thread running through the history of that curious craze. Transcending fads and fashions, tinsels have always attained an especial desirability, achieving a cult

Penny portrait by Park (1839), tinselled in the style associated with H. J. Webb [1920s?] (DP)

status shared only by domes of wax fruit. Admired by such esteemed company as the Sitwells, among whom Sacheverell identified theatrical prints in Mr Pollock's window as being part and parcel of 'the national genius';[37] Margaret Lambert and Enid Marx, who made much of them in their pioneering survey of *English Popular and Traditional Art* (1946); and James Laver, whose 1948 'Good Bad Art' article in *The Studio* is heralded by a tinselled Mr Horn as Caspar brandishing the eagle's wing. Barbara Jones included the original tinselled Richard III in her *Black Eyes and Lemonade* exhibition at the Whitechapel Art Gallery in 1951 (he staged a comeback appearance in 2004 when Sir John Soane's Museum went West) and Angus McBean not only collected them but also made his own. Margaret Lane wrote of E. P. Prior's collection that 'the sequin-like brilliance of the framed theatrical tinsels covering every inch of the walls, put one in mind of a casket of stage jewels',[38] and Mr May the theatrical costumier in Garrick Street, who supplied the Victorian foilstone tunics for Diaghilev's ballet *The Triumph of Neptune* in 1926,[39] used 'tinselled and other theatrical prints much as an average person uses wallpaper'.[40] Tinsels are prime examples of what may best be described as *Saturday Book* taste and were the stock-in-trade of such long-lost luminaries as Mr Block of Barter Street, Mr Lyon of the Court Bookshop, and Mr Meier of Cecil Court, in whose cluttered shop interior, as photographed by Edwin Smith, a pair of tinsels looms large.[41] The tradition is continued today by Mr Drummond, who still offers vintage tinsel pictures at Pleasures of Past Times, the last in the line of such establishments and one of *THE* shops of London.

Elevated above the tuppence coloured characters and scenes of the pasteboard drama, tinsel pictures are the crown jewels of an illusionary world of rampant romantic escapism, offering the ultimate, evocative theatrical echoes of the past. Firing the train of the imagination, these spangled stars on which the curtain never falls are best viewed by candlelight to emulate the flicker of the footlights. These dashing heroes and ravishing heroines, most of whom we know little of beyond their names, have yet achieved a glittering immortality. Striking the same stunning attitudes first seen in the reign of George IV, they stood steadfast against 'the vile tide of chromolithography' and emerged triumphant as English icons.[42]

Young Blood wishes to extend grateful thanks to the following people for assisting him with his enquiries: Roy Adams; Ian Anderson; Peter Baldwin; Stephen Calloway; Barbara Cavanagh; Barry Clarke; Beverley Cook of the Museum of London; David Drummond; John Foreman, The Broadsheet King; Cathy Haill of the Theatre Museum; Olivia Horsfall Turner; Veronica Horwell; Kate Irvine; Julie Anne Lambert of the John Johnson Collection, Bodleian Library; Dodie Masterman; Hope Mayo of Houghton Library, Harvard University; Sheila O'Connell of the British Museum; David Powell; David Robinson; Vera Rule; Laurie Webb; and the late George Speaight.

1. Henry Mayhew, 'Letter XXXVIII' in *The Morning Chronicle*, 25 February 1850. Rediscovered by E. P Thompson and Eileen Mayo, *The Unknown Mayhew: Selections from the 'Morning Chronicle' 1849–1850* (1971) and reprinted in full by Gerald Morice and George Speaight as 'New Light on the Juvenile Drama' in Theatre Notebook, xxvi (1971–72), pp. 115–121.

2. Infuriatingly, the original source of this description escapes me. Answer on a postcard please, or an email to horatioblood@yahoo.co.uk

3. George Speaight, *The History of the English Toy Theatre* (1969) [= Speaight], p. 129. Essential reading for any student of the juvenile drama, the chapter 'Portraits and Tinsel' includes many literary references not cited here.

4. An example of dubious vintage is illustrated in James Laver, *Stampe Popolari Inglesi* [1976], pl. 140.

5. For a seventeenth century English example see Sheila O'Connell, *The Popular Print in England 1550–1850* (1999), pl. III. Later manifestations are the gilded sheets of French *imagerie populaire* published by Pellerin of Epinal. Closer in kinship to theatrical tinsel perhaps were the gold embossed borders issued by Ackermann in the early nineteenth century.

6. See *Notes and Queries* cited by F. Gordon Roe, 'Prints and Tinsel' in *The Connoisseur*, April 1932.

7. The colour was painted on and brush marks are visible on surviving sheets of unstamped foil.

8. The other major publisher of eminently tinsellable portraits was Park.

9. The London trade directories reveal that his name was not Robert as previously thought.

10. To be sung to the tune of *The Calais Packet* (alias *Hunting the Hare*), a devilish difficult accomplishment.

11. In 'A Chat with a Christmas Card King' in *The British Empire Paper, Stationery & Printing Trades' Journal* (1908), Jonathan King recalled that such pieces of fabric were "cut out by pattern in blue paper, and shaded up." Some of these patterns survive in his collection at the Museum of London.

12. Further information on Brown will be found in my forthcoming monograph on the subject, *Tinsel Resplendent*.

13. A. E. Wilson, *Penny Plain, Two Pence Coloured* (1932) [= Wilson], p. 105, from information supplied by H. J. Webb.

14. A statement by H. J. Webb hints that the dies could have been made even as early as 1826. See David Powell, *W. G. Webb and the Victorian Toy Theatre* (2005) [= Powell], p. 24.

15. 'Penny Plain and Twopence Coloured. A Chat with Webb, the Miniature Theatre Maker' in *The Pall Mall Gazette*, July 24 1889. The tinsel book later passed to Harry Furniss, the black and white artist, and since 1953 has been in the Houghton Library, Harvard University, Massachusetts, USA.

16. Elkin Mathews Catalogue 153, Autumn 1953.

17. [J. F. Wilson], *A Few Personal Recollections, by an Old Printer* (1896) p. 38.

18. Jonathan King also had his own dies, a handful of which survive in the Museum of London.

19. John Ashton, 'Childhood's Drama' in *Varia* (1894).

20. 'A Chat with a Christmas Card King' (1908).

21. As advertised on his books of words.

22. According to an article in the *Evening News*, 1937. The copy I have seen is an undated fragment.

23. Puppets and scenes are profusely illustrated in Antonio Pasqualino, *L'opera dei pupi* (1977). I am indebted to Barry Clarke for drawing the similarities to my attention.

24. Speaight, p. 134.

25. Ashton, *Varia* (1894).

26. The film is available to view on www.pathe.com. In 1944, Pathé also filmed the Pollock sisters in the last days of Hoxton Street for *Model Theatre* (also known as *Penny Plain Twopence Coloured* or *The Young Idea*), and several years earlier Benjamin Pollock himself was filmed by Gaumont for their newsreel *Penny Plain – Twopence Coloured*.

27. Wilson, p. 105.

28. *The Studio*, December 1940.

29. Miss Lomax gave Victorian toy theatre performances in her antimacassared drawing room in Brighton to raise money for the war effort.

30. *Fifteenth Wartime Bulletin of The British Puppet & Model Theatre Guild*, [1944], p. 8.

31. *Op. cit.*

32. Speaight, p. 155.

33. H. J. Webb admitted the problems of obtaining tinsel in an interview for the *Daily Chronicle* in 1926. See Powell, p. 24.

34. Wilson, p. 105, says W. G. Webb; Speaight, p. 131, says James Webb.

35. Michael R. Booth (ed.), 'Fringes, Foil Paper, Spangles, Jewellery' in *Victorian Theatrical Trades Articles from The Stage 1883–1884* (1981).

36. They were knocked down to the Cotsen Children's Library, Princeton University, New Jersey, USA.

37. Sacheverell Sitwell, *British Architects and Craftsmen* (1945), p. 10.

38. Quoted in Speaight, p. 167.

39. David Powell, Historical Note to the 'Holt' reprint of *The Silver Palace* (2003).

40. F. Gordon Roe, 'Prints and Tinsel' in *The Connoisseur*, April 1932. Mr May's father Samuel was costumier to The Britannia Theatre, Hoxton.

41. Olive Cook and Edwin Smith, 'The One in the Window' in *The Saturday Book 9* (1949).

42. With acknowledgements to Mr Clarke.